SWEET

Vegan

TREATS

SWEET

Vegan

TREATS

90 RECIPES FOR COOKIES, BROWNIES, CAKES, AND TARTS

Hannah Kaminsky

Skyhorse Publishing

Skyhorse Publishing books may be purchased in bulk at special discounts for sales promotion, corporate gifts, fund-raising, or educational purposes. Special editions can also be created to specifications. For details, contact the Special Sales Department, Skyhorse Publishing, 307 West 36th Street, 11th Floor, New York, NY 10018 or info@skyhorsepublishing.com.

Skyhorse® and Skyhorse Publishing® are registered trademarks of Skyhorse Publishing, Inc.®, a Delaware corporation.

Visit our website at www.skyhorsepublishing.com.

10 9 8 7 6 5 4 3

Library of Congress Cataloging-in-Publication Data

Names: Kaminsky, Hannah, 1989- author.
Title: Sweet vegan treats: 90 cookies, brownies, cakes, tarts, and more
    baked goods / Hannah Kaminsky.
Description: New York, NY: Skyhorse Publishing, [2019]
Identifiers: LCCN 2019017622| ISBN 9781510741843 (print: alk. paper) | ISBN
    9781510741867 (ebook)
Subjects: LCSH: Desserts. | Vegan cooking. | LCGFT: Cookbooks.
Classification: LCC TX773 .K284 2019 | DDC 641.86—dc23 LC record available
    at https://lccn.loc.gov/2019017622

Cover design by Laura Klynstra
Cover photo by Hannah Kaminsky

Print ISBN: 978-1-5107-4184-3
Ebook ISBN: 978-1-5107-4186-7

Printed in China

Contents

Thank You!

Yes, you, reading these words right here and now! While it feels a bit contrived, if not disingenuous, to spray gratitude indiscriminately into the crowd like this, there's no easy way to express just how much your support means to me. Without a hungry and willing audience, which includes people like you, *Sweet Vegan Treats* would never have become a printed and published reality, let alone my other half-dozen cookbooks. It's unreal to look back on the original printing of *My Sweet Vegan* more than a decade ago and take stock of how drastically the landscape of food culture has shifted since then, and yet there's still a place on your shelf, be it physical or digital, for my work. That is why I want to thank you, first and foremost, for your enthusiasm, kindness, and hunger for a second serving of dessert.

A relic of antiquated baking techniques and largely untested theories, it's been a dream to bring the original concept back from the dead to give it new life as *Sweet Vegan Treats*. Not just a quick reprint, but a complete revival. So much has changed since the first printing, both in my approach to baking and the means available to the everyday cook, that this is an entirely new book. Key changes you'll find here include . . .

- **Less sugar!** Most important, a good dessert should emphasize flavor rather than straight-up sweetness.
- **No more corn syrup!** There are simply better alternatives available on the market and, as this controversial ingredient has fallen out of favor, it's become more difficult to locate, too.
- **Vegan butter instead of margarine!** Such high-quality options didn't exist over a decade ago and there's no need to pretend we like the flavor of those waxy, old-school fluorescent yellow sticks anymore.
- **More gluten-free and whole-grain options!** Dessert should be for everyone, no matter dietary restrictions. Most recipes that still use standard wheat flour can be adapted with a gluten-free blend as well.
- **New recipe names!** Sometimes, plain titles like "French Toast" just don't do the dish justice, or in the case of the Dark

Mocha Revelation Cake, "Devastation" suddenly struck me as downright antagonistic. Don't worry though, all your old favorites are still there.

If you've been baking along with me all this time, welcome back. If this is all sparkling new to you, grab an apron and roll up your sleeves; you're in for a real treat.

Introduction

Imagine, at the tender age of eighteen, suddenly having the opportunity to write, photograph, and publish your own cookbook fall right into your lap. Far from an expert, I had cut my teeth learning from trial and error—and error, and error. Unthinkable crazy talk, or perhaps pie in the sky, as it were! Watching *My Sweet Vegan* transform from a wild flight of fancy into a bound set of glossy pages felt surreal back in the day, just as every book that has come since then. *Sweet Vegan Treats* is the next chapter in this lifelong story.

Based on my earliest ventures in the kitchen as a new vegan and young adolescent, even I could have been convinced that eggs and dairy really are indispensable to delectable sweets. During my freshman year in high school, I churned out muffins and cookies more akin to cement doorstops than edible foodstuffs, but spurred on by a voracious sweet tooth, I never gave up. I was adamant that my creations would one day taste better than anything else on the market, vegan or otherwise. For that matter, it was unacceptable to serve a good *vegan* pastry; it needed to be delicious by any standards.

It hasn't all been smooth sailing. A fateful experiment in search of making vegan marshmallows immediately comes to mind as quite possibly my largest, and definitely stickiest, explosion to date. I'm not talking about a trivial spraying of the walls; marshmallow goop was all over the floor, stove, stuck inside door handles, dripping into drawers, in my hair, the whole nine yards. Then there was the ill-conceived salt-and-pepper ice cream that left me coughing and sneezing for days after a single, fateful scoop. Let's not forget about the white chocolate Bundt cake that might as well have been made of glue based on the texture of the crumb, or lack thereof.

Yet, through these spectacular failures, meltdowns, burnt edges, and towers of dirty dishes, I learned what works and what doesn't. Stubbornly reworking some recipes four, five, even six times, I gradually unlocked the "secrets" to produce foolproof, mouthwatering treats that everyone can appreciate.

It's easier and more delicious than ever to live without animal products now, as new alternatives and cruelty-free innovations are hitting mainstream awareness at lightning speed these days. Of course, that still doesn't mean you need

to *be* vegan to *eat* vegan; in my book, it's all just good food, no matter what you want to call it. Whether you're grappling with dietary restrictions, food allergies, ethical quandaries, or just have a serious sweet tooth, there's something here for you tucked within these colorful pages.

Happy Baking!

Ingredient Guide

Set yourself up for culinary success by stocking your pantry with the very best ingredients. If you ever get stuck while shopping, turn your search online, where most things, fresh, frozen, canned, and beyond, can be sent to your door with the click of a button.

Agar (Agar-Agar)

Also known as kanten, agar is a gelatinous substance made out of seaweed. It's a very close if not identical stand-in for traditional gelatin, which is extracted from the collagen within animals' connective tissues. Agar comes in powdered, flaked, and stick form. I prefer to use the powder because it dissolves more easily and measures teaspoon for teaspoon like standard gelatin. However, if you can only find the flakes, just whiz them in a spice grinder for a few minutes, and voilà—instant agar powder! Agar can be found in Asian markets and some health food stores.

Agave Nectar

Derived from the same plant as tequila but far less potent, this syrup is made from the condensed juice found at the core of the agave cactus. It is available in both light and dark varieties—the dark possesses a more nuanced, complex, and somewhat floral flavor, while the light tends to provide only a clean sweetness. Considered a less refined form of sugar, agave nectar has a much lower glycemic index than many traditional granulated sweeteners and is therefore consumed by some diabetics in moderation.

All-Purpose Flour

While wonderful flours can be made from all sorts of grains, beans, nuts, and seeds, the gold standard in everyday baking and cooking is still traditional "all-purpose" wheat flour. Falling texturally somewhere in between cake flour and bread flour, it works as a seamless binder, strong foundation, and neutral base. It's an essential pantry staple for me, stocked in my cupboard at all times. All-purpose flour may be labeled in stores as unbleached white flour or simply "plain flour." Gluten-free all-purpose flour is also widely available now in mainstream markets and can be substituted at a 1:1 ratio for those sensitive to wheat. Many different blends exist, but I've personally had good results with Bob's

Red Mill®, Cup 4 Cup®, and King Arthur®. If you'd like to whip up your own blend, that's also easy enough as long as you have a well-stocked pantry.

All-Purpose Gluten-Free Flour Blend

6 cups white rice flour

2 cups potato starch or cornstarch

1 cup tapioca flour

2 tablespoons xanthan gum

Simply whisk all the dry goods together until thoroughly mixed. Store in an airtight container and measure out as needed. If the recipe you're following already calls for xanthan gum, you can omit it since it's included in this blend.

Almond Meal / Flour

Almond flour is nothing more than raw almonds ground down into a fine powder, light and even in consistency which makes it ideal for baking, while almond meal is generally a bit coarser. To make your own, just throw a pound or so of completely unadulterated almonds into your food processor, and pulse until floury. It's helpful to freeze the almonds in advance so that they don't overheat and turn into almond butter. You can also create a finer texture by passing the initial almond meal through a fine sieve to sift out the larger pieces. Due to their high oil content, ground nuts can go rancid fairly quickly. If you opt to stock up and save some for later, be sure to store the freshly ground almond flour in an airtight container in the refrigerator or freezer. To cut down on labor and save a little time, almond flour or meal can be purchased in bulk from natural food stores.

Apple Cider Vinegar

As with oil, vinegar may originate from different types of produce, and the flavor will vary depending upon the source. Thinking along these lines, apple cider vinegar could be considered the olive oil of vinegars—flavorful, useful, and an all-around great thing to have on hand. Regular white wine vinegar or the other standard options would certainly *work,* but the distinctive flavor of apple cider vinegar rounds out baked goods so perfectly, and it is so easy to find . . . why wouldn't you use it?

Aquafaba

It's the not-so-secret ingredient taking the world by storm, dubbed a "miracle" by some and a food science breakthrough by others. In case you're not already a fervent fan, aquafaba is the excess liquid found in any ordinary can of chickpeas. Technically, any bean can produce aquafaba, but the unique ratios of protein and starch found in garbanzo beans has been found to best mimic the unique binding and whipping properties previously only seen in egg whites. Different brands will yield slightly different results, but I've never found any that are complete duds. For more delicate applications like meringues or marshmallow fluff, you can always concentrate your aquafaba to create a stronger foam matrix by cooking it gently over the stove and reducing some of the water.

Arrowroot Powder / Flour

Thanks to arrowroot, you can thicken sauces, puddings, and mousses with ease. This white powder is very similar to kudzu and is often compared to other starchy flours. However, arrowroot is so fine that it produces much smoother results, and is less likely to stick together and form large, glutinous lumps when baking. In a pinch, cornstarch can be an adequate substitute, but I highly recommend seeking out arrowroot. Most grocery stores have a brand or two tucked in among the spices in the baking aisle.

Black Cocoa Powder

What do you get when you oxidize Dutch-process cocoa powder to the extreme? Black cocoa, dark as coal, certainly lives up to its name and produces amazing color in baked goods. However, it has a much lower fat content than standard cocoa and should therefore be used sparingly to avoid altering the texture of your baked goods. In a pinch, feel free to substitute regular Dutch-process cocoa for an equally tasty, if comparatively paler, dessert.

Black Salt (Kala Namak)

Lovingly if crudely nicknamed "fart salt" around these parts, the sulfurous odor released by a big bagful really does smell like . . . well, you can probably guess. Despite that unpromising introduction, it does taste far better, and eerily similar to eggs. Enhancing everything from tofu scrambles to loaves of challah, it's one of those secret ingredients that every vegan should have in their arsenal. Don't let the name confuse you though; the fine grains are actually mottled pink in appearance, not black.

Brown Rice Syrup

Caramel-colored and thick like honey, brown rice syrup is a natural sweetener that is produced via the fermentation of brown rice. It tastes less sweet than granulated sugar, adding a wholesome complexity to baked goods. The deep flavor of brown rice syrup is best cast in supporting roles, complementing other aspects of the dish without taking center stage.

Butter

It's a basic kitchen staple, but good dairy-free butter can be quite elusive if you don't know what to look for. Some name brands contain whey or other milk derivatives, while others conceal the elusive, animal-derived Vitamin D_3, so be alert when scanning ingredient labels. For ease, I prefer to use it in stick format, such as Earth Balance® Buttery Sticks or Miyoko's Kitchen European Style Cultured VeganButter. Never try to substitute spreadable butter from a tub! These varieties have much more water to allow them to spread while cold, and will thus bake and cook differently. I always use unsalted butter unless otherwise noted, but you are welcome to use salted as long as you remove about ¼ teaspoon of salt per ¼ cup of butter from the recipe. Overly salted food is one of the first flaws that diners notice, so take care with your seasoning and always adjust to taste.

Cacao Nibs

Also known as raw chocolate, cacao nibs are unprocessed cacao nuts, simply broken up into smaller pieces. Much more bitter and harsh than the sweet, mellow chocolate found in bars or chips, it is often used for texture and accent flavor in desserts. Sometimes it can be found coated in sugar to soften its inherent acidity, but for baking, you want the plain, raw version if possible. Seek out bags of cacao nibs in health food stores; if you're really lucky, you may be able to find them in the bulk bins of well-stocked specialty stores.

Chia Seeds

Yes, this is the same stuff that makes Chia Pets so green and fuzzy, and yes, the seeds are edible! Tiny but mighty, what makes these particular seeds so special is that they form a gel when mixed with liquid. This makes them a powerful binder when trying to replace eggs, or should flaxseeds be in short supply. Store in the freezer for a longer life span, and grind them before using in baked goods to maintain an even crumb texture.

Chocolate

Why does something so common, so beloved and easily accessible, need further explanation? Chocolate is chocolate, especially when you're reaching for the dark stuff, right? Many name brands that prefer quantity to quality would beg to differ. Obviously, white and milk chocolate are out of the picture, yet some dark, bittersweet, and semisweet chocolates still don't make the vegan cut. Even those that claim to be "70% cacao solids, extra-special dark" may have milk solids or butterfat lurking within. Don't buy the hype or the filler! Stay vigilant and check all labels to uncover superior flavor undiluted by dairy products.

Chocolate Crème-Filled Sandwich Cookies

As America's favorite cookie, it is no surprise that the Oreo® would come up sooner or later on this list. While the original Oreo® has changed its ways to take out the trans fats and animal products, there are many other options on the market. Newman's Own makes an organic version that tastes just like the cookies you might remember from your childhood. Trader Joe's even has their own house brand, always available at a very reasonable price and sometimes in exciting seasonal varieties. Any wafer cookies with a vanilla filling will do, or you can even whip up your own by combining the Chocolate Wafer Cookie recipe on page 229 with the vanilla frosting recipe from the Root Beer Float Cupcakes on page 149.

Chocolate Wafer Cookie Crumbs

Simply flat, crunchy cocoa cookies, there are quite a few vegan options on the market. I typically use the Alphabet Cookies from Newman's Own, but plenty of other brands will work just as well. Just be sure to check the ingredient statement, and stay away from those that look soft or chewy. For a thrifty endeavor, you could also try baking your own at home with the Chocolate Wafer Cookie recipe on page 229! Once baked and fully cooled, pulverize the cookies into crumbs using a food processor, blender, or a good old-fashioned rubber mallet, depending upon your mood.

Cocoa Butter

Chocolate is comprised of two key elements: The cocoa solids, which give it that distinct cocoa flavor, and the cocoa butter, which is the fat that provides the body. Cocoa butter is solid at room temperature, like all tropical oils, so it's best to measure it after melting, as the firm chunks can appear deceptively voluminous. It's really important to pick up high quality, food-grade cocoa butter. As a popular ingredient in body lotions and lip balms, some offerings come with fillers and undesirable additives, so shop carefully if you search locally. Also avoid deodorized cocoa butter, unless you'd rather omit its natural flavor from your desserts.

Coconut Milk

When called for in this book, I'm referring to regular, full-fat coconut milk. That fat is necessary for a smooth, creamy mouthfeel and richer taste. In ice cream, light coconut milk cannot be substituted without detrimental effects to the final texture. Plain coconut milk is found canned in the ethnic foods aisle of the grocery store. You can make it yourself from fresh coconut meat, but in most cases, such as baking and general dessert-making when it's not the featured flavor, the added hassle honestly isn't worth the expense or effort.

Coconut Oil

Once demonized as artery-clogging sludge not fit to grease a doorframe, nutritionists now can't recommend this tropical fat highly enough. Touted for its benefits when consumed or used topically, it's readily available just about anywhere you turn. Two varieties populate store shelves: Virgin (or raw/unrefined) coconut oil and refined coconut oil. Virgin gets the best press from the health experts since it's less processed, and it bears the subtle aroma of the coconut flesh. Refined has been deodorized and is essentially flavorless, allowing it to blend seamlessly with any other flavors. They both solidify below 76°F, but virgin oil reaches its smoke point at 350°F while refined is at 450°F. Either works fine for raw or unbaked treats, but I would recommend refined for baked applications.

Confectioners' Sugar

Otherwise known as powdered sugar, icing sugar, or 10x sugar, confectioners' sugar is a very finely ground version of standard white sugar with just a touch of cornstarch added to prevent clumping. If you should reach into your pantry and come out empty-handed, you can make your own by combining 1 cup of granulated sugar with 1 tablespoon of cornstarch in your food processor or spice grinder. Simply blend on the highest speed for about two minutes, allowing the dust to settle before opening your machine up—unless you want to inhale a cloud of sugar!

Cream Cheese

Many innovative companies now make dairy-free products that will give you the most authentic shmears and cream cheese frostings imaginable. These soft spreads also hold up beautifully in cookie dough and piecrusts, contributing a great tangy flavor and excellent structure. My favorite brands are Tofutti®, Kite Hill®, and Miyoko's®, but there are even more options in ample supply at well-stocked natural foods markets. You can even make your own from scratch with relative ease using the recipe on page 230, but bear in mind that it will likely produce a coarser texture than anything store-bought.

Cream of Tartar

Don't let the name fool you; cream of tartar has absolutely nothing to do with either cream nor tartar sauce. It's actually created through the fermentation process that grapes undergo in the production of wine. Thus, it can contribute a good deal of acid to recipes in very small doses. Sometimes used as a stabilizer, it can create flavors similar to buttermilk, or be used to create baking powder: For a small batch, sift together 2 tablespoons cream of tartar with 1 tablespoon baking soda and 1 teaspoon cornstarch.

Flavor Extracts

I usually try to stay as far away from flavor extracts as possible, because they are all too often artificial, insipid, and a poor replacement for the real thing. However, vanilla (see page 12 for further details), peppermint, and almond are my main exceptions, as high-quality extracts from the actual sources are readily available in most markets. Just make sure to avoid any bottles that list sugar, corn syrup, colors, or chemical stabilizers in addition to your flavor of choice. For more unconventional essences, if your supermarket searches end up unsuccessful, try the internet. I've found OliveNation.com in particular to be a reliable resource.

Flaxseeds

Ground flaxseeds make an excellent vegan egg-replacer when combined with water. One tablespoon of the whole seeds produces approximately 1½ tablespoons of the ground powder. While you can purchase pre-ground flaxseed meal in many stores, I prefer to grind them fresh for each recipe, as they tend to go rancid much more quickly once broken down. Not to mention, it takes mere seconds to powder your own flaxseeds in a spice grinder. If you do opt to purchase flax meal instead, be sure to store the powder in your refrigerator or freezer until you are ready to use it. These tiny seeds can be found in bulk bins and prepackaged in the baking aisle of natural food stores.

Garbanzo Bean (Chickpea) Flour

Gaining in popularity as a versatile gluten-free flour, garbanzo flour is just what you might imagine; nothing but dried, finely ground chickpeas. When used in baking, it can be used as a substitute for about 20–25 percent of the wheat flour called for in a recipe or to add a toothsome density to cakes or cookies. It can also be cooked with water like polenta, and eaten either as a hot porridge or let set overnight in a baking dish, sliced, and then fried to make what is called chickpea panisse. Just be warned that eaten raw (if, say, someone decided to sample raw cookie batter that contains garbanzo flour) it is very bitter and unpleasant.

Garbanzo flour should be readily available in most grocery stores in the baking or natural foods section, but if you have a powerful blender like a Vitamix (see Kitchen Toys and Tools) with a dry grinding container, you can make your own from dried, split chickpeas (also known as chana dal). Process 2 cups of legumes at a time, and use the plunger to keep things

moving. Once finely ground, let the dust settle for a few minutes before removing the lid of the container.

Graham Crackers

When I first went searching for vegan graham crackers, I was appalled at my lack of options. Why every brand in sight needed to include honey was beyond me. So, what is an intrepid food enthusiast to do in a tight situation like this? Shop, search, and browse some more, of course. Concealed among the rest, and often in natural foods stores, there are a few brands that exclude all animal products. Believe it or not, some of the best options are the store-brand, no-name biscuits that may otherwise get overlooked. Keep your eyes peeled for unexpected steals and deals. Go the extra mile and make your own from scratch using the recipe on page 235 for a truly superlative staple, but make twice as much as you'll need for the final recipe, because you'll want to snack on those all by themselves.

Graham Flour

Best known in the form of crackers, graham flour is simply a fancy type of wheat flour. It is made from a process that separates all parts of the wheat kernel itself and recombines them in different proportions. For reasons beyond my grasp, this unique flour is not sold in all countries. If you are having a hard time getting your hands on some, and don't mind a treat with a slightly different, denser texture, regular old whole wheat flour can be substituted. With a little bit more effort, you can fabricate a closer approximation of the wholesome flavor and coarse grind with ¾ cup plus 2 tablespoons whole wheat pastry flour and 2 tablespoons toasted wheat germ.

Granulated Sugar

Yes, that's plain old, regular white sugar I'm talking about. Surprised to see this most basic sweetener here? It's true that all sugar (beet or cane) is derived from plant sources and therefore vegan by nature. However, there are some sneaky things going on behind the scenes in big corporations these days. Some cane sugar is filtered using bone char, a very non-vegan process, but that will never be specified on a label. The same goes for brown sugar as well, which is really just white sugar with molasses added back in. If you're not sure about the brand that you typically buy, your best bet is to contact the manufacturer directly and ask.

To bypass this problem, many vegans purchase unbleached cane sugar. While it is a suitable substitute, unbleached cane sugar does have a higher molasses content than white sugar, so it has more of a brown sugar–like flavor, and tends to produce desserts that are denser. Luckily, there are a few caring companies that go to great pains to ensure the purity of their sugar products, such as Florida Crystals® and Amalgamated Sugar Company®, the suppliers to

White Satin, Fred Meyer, Western Family, and Parade. You can often find appropriate sugar in health food store bulk bins these days to save some money, but as always, verify the source before forking over the cash. As sugar can be a touchy vegan subject, it is best to use your own judgment when considering which brand to purchase.

Instant Coffee Powder or Granules

Though generally unfit for drinking as intended, instant coffee is an ideal way to add those crave-worthy roasted, smoky notes to any recipe without also incorporating a lot of extra liquid. Stored in a dry, dark place, a small jar should last a long time. You can even find decaf versions, in case you're more sensitive to caffeine but still want that flavor in your recipes. I prefer powder to granules because it dissolves more easily, but both can work interchangeably with a bit of vigorous mixing.

Instant Potato Flakes

Instant mashed potatoes have been a convenient pantry staple since the 1920s when semi-homemade shortcuts were all the rage. Larded with waxy processed fats, dried dairy products, and aggressive doses of salt, these are not the kind of "quick fix" side dishes I can endorse. Rather, I'm looking for just the plain, unadorned flakes of dehydrated potatoes, ready to be reconstituted with hot water and mixed up into any variety of recipe applications. Though rather bland by themselves, that's precisely what makes them so versatile. You're more likely to encounter them in health food stores or online shops, either in large packages or bulk bins. Just make sure there's nothing else added, and that they are in fact flakes, not granules, since the two formats absorb liquid at a different rate.

Maple Syrup

One of my absolute favorite sweeteners, there is simply no substitute for real, 100 percent maple syrup. Of course, this incredible indulgence does come at a hefty price. Though it would be absolute sacrilege to use anything but authentic Grade B maple syrup on pancakes or waffles in my house, I will sometimes bend the rules in recipes where it isn't such a prominent flavor, in order to save some money. In these instances, I'll substitute a maple-agave blend, which still carries the flavor from the actual source, but bulks it up with an equal dose of agave for sweetening power. Grade A is a fine substitute in a pinch, but contrary to what the letter would suggest, it's surprisingly less flavorful than Grade B.

Matcha

Perhaps one of my all-time favorite flavorings, matcha is a very high-quality powdered green tea. It is used primarily in Japanese tea ceremonies and can have an intense, complex, and bitter taste when used in large amounts. Contrary to what many new bakers think, this is *not* the same as the green tea leaves you'll find in mega mart tea bags! Those are vastly inferior in the

flavor department, and real matcha is ground much finer. There are many levels of quality, with each step up in grade carrying a higher price tag. Because it can become quite pricey, I would suggest buying a mid-range or "culinary" grade, which should be readily available at any specialty tea store and many health food markets.

Nondairy Milk

The foundation of many cream and custard pies, I kept this critical ingredient somewhat ambiguous for a reason. Most types of nondairy milk will work in these recipes, and I wouldn't want to limit anyone with specific allergies. The only type that I absolutely do not recommend using is rice milk, as it tends to be much thinner, often gritty, and completely lacking in the body necessary to make rich, satisfying desserts. Unless explicitly specified, any other type of vegan milk substitute will work. My top pick is unsweetened almond milk because it tends to be a bit thicker, richer, and still has a neutral flavor. Don't be afraid to experiment, though; there's a lot to choose from!

Nutritional Yeast

Unlike active yeast, nutritional yeast is not used to leaven baked goods, but to flavor all sorts of dishes. Prized for its distinctly cheesy flavor, it's a staple in most vegan pantries and is finally starting to gain recognition in mainstream cooking as well. Though it is almost always found in savory recipes, I sometimes like to add a tiny pinch to some desserts, bringing out its subtle buttery characteristics. It can be found either in the baking aisle or in many bulk bin sections.

Olive Oil

One of the most sweeping changes in these revamped recipes was replacing all the canola oil with olive oil. Though canola is king for neutral flavor, it's become a bit controversial for some when it comes to health and environmental impact. I've always been a much bigger fan of olive oil anyhow, and after a bit of experimentation, I found that it could seamlessly fill those shoes, despite the common misconceptions over how it might ruin the delicate flavors in cakes or other sweet treats. Simply opt for a "light" variety to reduce the stronger, grassier, or more peppery notes. This type of olive oil is also processed in a way that makes it almost colorless and better for high-heat applications than extra virgin, for instance.

Truth be told, my absolute favorite oils for baking are avocado oil and rice bran oil, in that order, but I understand that these aren't as widely available. If you have the access and inclination, though, give either a try for an upgraded option.

Puffed Grains

Those crispy rice cereals that have graced breakfast tables for over 50 years are all too familiar, but what about the other puffed grains, such as barley, wheat, or millet? Yes, the exact same process can be used on all of these staples to create light, crunchy cereal grains, each with their own distinctive flavors and shapes. Puffed quinoa and millet, called for in the Power-Hungry Granola (page 51), are two of the more unusual puffed grains in my breakfast bowl, but either can be replaced with crispy rice cereal in an equal proportion. I prefer to stick with plain grains when making granola. Boxed cereals that have sugar added are fine too, just expect a sweeter result, or dial down the sugar in the recipe to compensate. Most health food stores will stock more uncommon varieties in bulk bins, but feel free to experiment with whatever is easiest for you to obtain.

Sour Cream

Another creative alternative comes to the rescue of vegan bakers everywhere! Vegan sour cream provides an amazingly similar yet dairy-free version of the original tangy spread. In a pinch, I suppose you might be able to get away with using "Greek" style vegan yogurt instead, but it doesn't have the same richness and body, so the resulting desserts may be a bit less decadent. Vegan sour cream can often be found neatly tucked in among its dairy-based rivals in the grocery store, or with the other refrigerated dairy alternatives. The soy-based Sour Supreme from Tofutti® remains my favorite, even over a decade of baking experience later.

Sprinkles

What's a birthday party without a generous handful of sprinkles to brighten up the cake?

Though these colorful toppers are made primarily of edible wax, they are often coated in confectioners' glaze, which is code for mashed-up insects, to give them their lustrous shine. Happily, you can now find specifically vegan sprinkles (sold as "Sprinkelz") produced by the Let's Do...® company, in both chocolate and colored versions, which can be found at just about any natural food store.

If you're feeling colorful, you can also make a healthier, sugar-free version with . . . amaranth! That's right; just plain old amaranth soaked in plant-based dyes and dehydrated will do the trick, since these toppers should be applied sparingly and don't contribute any discernable flavor. All you need to do is soak amaranth in a colorful liquid for 4 hours, drain, and bake for 50 to 60 minutes at 200°F, stirring every 10 minutes or so, until dry to the touch. Your dyeing guide is as follows:

- Beet juice for red/pink
- Turmeric with water for yellow
- Matcha with water for green

Use just enough liquid to cover the grains and ratios as desired to reach the shade you'd like, but bear in mind they won't be as brilliant as anything store-bought or chemically enhanced. Variations on these colors are easily blended, but this mix tends to do just fine for that extra touch of whimsy. Bake in separate batches until completely dry to prevent the colors from bleeding.

Store in an airtight container until ready to sprinkle in some fun!

Tahini

A staple of Middle Eastern cuisine, most grocery stores should be able to accommodate your tahini requests. Tahini is a paste very much like peanut butter, but it is made from sesame seeds rather than nuts. If you don't have any on hand and a trip to the market is not in your immediate plans, then any other nut butter will provide exactly the same texture within a recipe, though it will impart a different overall taste.

Textured Vegetable (or Soy) Protein

Typically shortened to the abbreviation of TVP (or TSP), this is a very concentrated protein, and a by-product of making soybean oil. It's consequently low in fat, and well-known for its appearances in savory dishes as a very convincing meat replacement. Cut into chunks, the spongy texture of TVP is especially receptive to other flavors and seasonings. This may sound like a strange ingredient to include within a book about sweet recipes, but like tofu, it has a fairly neutral flavor and can be seasoned in any way you can imagine! Bags or tubs of TVP are available in most health food stores and some bulk bin sections. Soy Curls® have a similar texture but are made from the whole soybean, if you would prefer a more complete protein. These come in longer strips, so simply pulse them in your blender or food processor to break them into a coarse, pebble-like consistency before proceeding with the recipe.

Tofu

Yes, I bake with tofu and I *don't* apologize for it! It lends fabulous moisture, structure, and even a punch of protein! When I use tofu in desserts, I always reach for the aseptic, shelf-stable packs made by Mori-Nu®. Not only do they seem to last indefinitely when unopened, they also blend down into a flawlessly smooth puree when processed thoroughly. These compact little boxes are all over the place in natural food stores and Asian markets, as well as online. Water-packed tofu sold in the produce section of standard grocery stores will have a much looser texture when baked and is likely to have a more "beany" flavor.

Turbinado Sugar

Coarse, light brown granulated sugar, it's hard to resist the sparkle that this edible glitter lends when applied to the outside of cookies. Though it's not the best choice for actually baking with since the large crystals make for an uneven distribution of sweetness, it adds a satisfying crunch and eye-appeal when used as decoration.

Vanilla (Extract, Paste, and Beans)

One of the most important ingredients in a baker's arsenal, vanilla is found in countless forms and qualities. It goes without saying that artificial flavorings pale in comparison to the real thing. Madagascar vanilla is the traditional full-bodied vanilla that most people appreciate in desserts, so stick with that and you can't go wrong. To take your desserts up a step, vanilla paste brings in the same amount of flavor, but includes those lovely little vanilla bean flecks that makes everyone think you busted out the good stuff and used whole beans. Vanilla paste can be substituted 1:1 for vanilla extract. Like whole vanilla beans, save the paste for things where you'll really see those specks of vanilla goodness, like ice creams, custards, and frostings. Vanilla beans, the most costly but flavorful option, can be used instead, at about 1 bean per 2 teaspoons of extract or paste.

Once you've split and scraped out the insides, get the most for your money by stashing the pod in a container of granulated sugar, to slowly infuse the sugar with delicious vanilla flavor. Or, just store the pod in a container until it dries out, and then grind it up very finely in a high-speed blender and use it to augment a good vanilla extract. The flavor won't be as strong as the seeds, but it does contribute to the illusion that you've used the good stuff.

Vegan Eggnog

Made with neither dairy nor eggs, commercially prepared vegan "eggnog" is actually quite delicious, contrary to what thoughts the name may evoke. It is a bit thinner than the traditional egg- and cream-based drink, but this actually makes it even better to bake with, as it doesn't tend to weigh cakes down nearly as much. Due to its seasonality, vegan "eggnog" is only available in the months surrounding Christmas, but during those times you should be able to find it in most mainstream marketplaces. Or you can make your own with a quick online search.

Wasabi Paste and Powder

Just like the mounds of green paste served with sushi, the prepared wasabi paste found in tubes is almost certainly not made of wasabi root. Strange but true, it's typically colored horseradish instead, due to the rarity and expense of real wasabi. Read labels carefully, because it's one of those things that seems guaranteed to be vegan-friendly, but can give you a nasty surprise if you're not careful. Milk derivatives are often added, for reasons I couldn't begin to explain. The potent flavor dissipates over time, so be sure to toss any that has been sitting in your pantry well past its prime. If quality paste is nowhere to be found, opt for prepared horseradish (blended only with a dash of vinegar) instead. In some cases, mustard powder can lend a similar flavor instead of wasabi powder, but only in very small doses.

White Whole Wheat Flour

Look out, whole wheat pastry flour, healthy bakers everywhere have a new best friend! It may look and taste like regular white flour, but is instead milled from the whole grain. Simply made from hard white wheat berries instead of red, the color and flavor is much lighter, making it the perfect addition to nearly every sort of baking application you can think of. If you're concerned about getting more fiber into your diet, feel free to switch out the all-purpose flour in any recipe in this book for white whole wheat.

Whole Wheat Pastry Flour

I just love using whole wheat flour whenever possible, to add in some extra fiber and nutrients, but all too often it can make desserts dense and unpalatable. This is where whole wheat pastry flour steps in! It has a lower gluten content and is therefore less likely to create that tough, heavy texture typically associated with the wholesome grain. White whole wheat flour can also be used for the same applications.

Yogurt

No longer just soy, there are now flavors like coconut, almond, cashew, and beyond, there's a nut or a grain for everyone! Unless specified, opt for plain yogurt, rather than "Greek" style, which will be considerably thicker. I prefer to purchase the larger containers and weigh or measure out the requisite amount, since single-serving cups can vary in size. I'm quite partial to the almond-based version made by Kite Hill® but the "cashewgurt" from Forager® is a close second.

Tools of the Trade

Working with a scant arsenal of bare essentials at your disposal, all you really need is a mixing bowl, big wooden spoon, measuring cups, and a couple of baking tins to whip up countless fabulous baked goods. Nonetheless, a few pieces of supplemental equipment will make your time in the kitchen pass much more quickly and efficiently, improve your end results, and offer the ability to produce some more adventurous recipes. Below is a quick primer on the indispensable gadgets you'll find powering my culinary creations:

Baking Pans / Baking Dishes

There are a wide variety of baking dishes on the market—aluminum, nonstick, glass, silicone, and so on—but any type will generally work, as long as it is the size that the recipe calls for. Just make sure to give your baking pans a little extra attention in the greasing stage if they are not nonstick. Whenever I can, I use nonstick aluminized steel, but bakeware material is greatly a matter of personal preference, so this small detail is not terribly important. For the most part, all the baking pan shapes and sizes

mentioned in this book can be easily found in any good kitchen store, supermarket, or online.

Blender

They come in all shapes and sizes, with wildly varying prices to match. If you want the sturdiest machine that will grant you the most pureeing power, I can't recommend the Vitamix® highly enough. Yes, it's one of the priciest models on the market for consumer purchase, but it actually is professional quality and will pay for itself through saved time and aggravation. There is simply nothing else that can blend whole nuts so silky smooth, or grind whole beans down to perfectly fine flour. I use mine almost every day, whether for baking adventures or just blending myself a smoothie.

Broiler

If you've never used it before, you're missing out on one of the best elements built right into your oven. It reaches scorching-hot temperatures in seconds, providing instant firepower when you want to quickly brown surfaces or finish a dish with a touch of char. You can also use the broiler in toaster ovens for greater efficiency, since less heat is lost in smaller, more confined space. Set the rack as close to the heating element as possible to maximize that intensity and exposure. Unlike baking, broiling is most effective when the door to the oven is left slightly ajar to prevent steam from building up, preventing a proper dry sear.

Cookie Cutters

I do not use cookie cutters very often, as they can be a pain to work with. However, when necessary, I reach for big plastic ones, which are free of small details. Shapes that are too intricate tend to spread out into one big blob while cooking. Just because they make them doesn't mean they always work out well! Also, if I have the option, I stay far away from the metal cutters, as they tend to deform and rust rather easily. But, if that is all you can find, or you would rather stick with the metal, more power to you!

Food Processor

They both have a spinning blade at the bottom of a sealed canister, but don't consider a blender and a food processor as being interchangeable in every procedure. There's no way you'd be able to make pastry dough in a blender, but my food processor is the secret to effortlessly whipping up everything from silky-smooth hummus to flaky crust. If you have a limited budget for only one serious appliance investment, go for a food processor. Choose a model with at least 7–8 cups capacity, or else be prepared to process many recipes in batches.

Kitchen Torch

Hasn't every child wanted their own flame-thrower growing up? Okay, maybe I was just an odd child, but there's no denying the allure of playing with fire. A kitchen torch allows you that thrill with a bit more safety. Found in kitchen supply and specialty shops, these devices look somewhat like small guns and are powered by butane. Very reasonably priced at $10–$20 for most basic models, they make brûléeing or browning meringue a breeze.

Mandoline

No relation to the mandolin, a stringed musical instrument that resembles a banjo, the mandoline is the secret to deconstructing produce into perfect paper-thin slices, all the exact same width, without needing to pick up a knife. The frame can be made of plastic or metal and comes with numerous inserts that will adjust the width of the finished slices. Some even come with specialty attachments that will create waffle cuts and crinkle cuts, ideal for fancy French fries. A common misconception is that they're dangerous, but this only rings true when used improperly, like any other tool. Never, ever, *ever* operate a mandoline without the hand guard. I know far too many people, including myself, that have nearly lost fingers trying to beat the system and go it alone. That one last tiny slice off the bottom of that slippery potato just isn't worth the pain.

Microwave

Did you know that the first microwave ever built was 6 feet tall, weighed 750 pounds, and cost $5,000? Vast technological advances have significantly brought down all those figures, allowing the machines to become ubiquitous kitchen staples today. Few people give their microwaves a second thought, but different models can vary greatly in power and capacity. The average electromagnetic oven has an output of 700 watts, which is what most recipes are written to accommodate. If you're not sure about your own microwave, place a cup of water in a dish and see how long it takes to boil. For a 700-watt model, it should take about 2½ minutes; 1,000 watts will get you there in only 1¾ minutes. Rarely will you encounter a non-commercial machine that pumps out over 1,200 watts, which will boil water in under 1½ minutes. Once you harness the full power of your machine, adjust your cooking times accordingly. You can also find a more thorough conversion chart at MicrowaveWatt.com.

Piping / Pastry Bags and Tips

The very first time I picked up a piping bag to frost a cupcake, I knew that there was no going back. It just makes for a more professional presentation than frosting blobbed on with a knife, in my opinion. Piping bags are by no means necessary tools, but rather a baker's luxury. If you don't know how to wield a pastry bag or cannot be bothered with the hassle, there is no need to run out and buy one. However, should you wish to give piping a try, don't skimp on the quality! Piping bags come in heavy-duty, reusable fabric, or plastic and disposable varieties, which range in quality. This is one time when I like to use disposable, because piping bags really are a nightmare to clean. Just avoid the cheaper plastic bags, as they are often too thin to stand up to the pressure. As for the tips, you only need one or two big star tips to make immaculate swirls. You can also pipe straight out of the bag for a rounded spiral.

Silicone Baking Mats

I simply adore these flat, nonstick mats and use them at every opportunity. Likened to reusable parchment paper, they cut down on the cost and excess waste of traditional single-use fibers. In terms of performance, they also tend to reduce browning, so it's more difficult (but by no means impossible) to burn cookies when using them. While one should last you several years, it is helpful to have a few on hand. For best care, wash them promptly after each use with mild soap and a soft sponge. Never use a knife directly on these mats because they will slice through, indestructible though they may seem! Silpats® are the brand you're most likely to encounter, but plenty of alternatives can be located at any good kitchen supply store.

Spice Grinder

Otherwise known as a coffee grinder, this miniature appliance is so inexpensive and efficient that every home cook should have one! Spice grinders are perfect for quickly grinding nuts, seeds, grains, and, of course, spices, into a fine powder. Think of it as a mini food processor that can handily tackle smaller batches.

Spiralizer

Once an esoteric uni-tasking tool used exclusively in raw cuisine, spiralizers have taken the whole world by storm, spinning out curly strands of vegetables with a twist of the wrist. Operated much like a hand-crank pencil sharpener, firm fruits and vegetables can be spun through a series of small blades to make "noodles" or ribbons of various sizes. Zucchini are typically the gateway for more daring plant-based pasta facsimiles; I've had wonderful results with seedless cucumbers, carrots, beets, strips of pumpkin, daikon, and parsnips, to name a few. You can find spiralizers sold for $15–40, and you really don't need to splurge on this small investment, since they're really more or less just as effective. If you're still not quite ready to commit, you can get a similar sort of result from a julienne peeler, but it will take a bit more time and labor to turn out the same volume of skinny strands.

Springform Pan

Springform pans are a must for creating perfect cheesecakes. As opposed to standard cake pans, these flexible vessels boast removable sides, which allow softer cakes to remain intact when presented. Springform pans are relatively inexpensive and can be found in most food and kitchen stores, among the wide selection of baking pans. They are easily recognizable by a clamp on one side.

Stand Mixer

While hand mixers get the job done, a good stand mixer will save your arm a tremendous amount of grief. A high-quality stand mixer can cost a pretty penny, but it is usually worth its weight in gold. It is easy to multitask while this powerful and independent machine works its magic. If your kitchen space or budget doesn't allow for this luxury, then a hand mixer, or even the vigorous use of a whisk, will suit whenever a stand mixer is noted.

Strainer

When I call for one of these in a recipe, chances are I'm not talking about a pasta colander, with its large, spread-out holes. To sieve out raspberry seeds, drain canned beans, or take care of any other liquid/solid separation jobs, a decent fine-mesh sieve will tackle the job with ease. Seek out strainers with solid construction, so that the mesh won't pull out after repeated pressings with a spatula. One about 7–9 inches in diameter should accommodate.

Essential Techniques

Mastering a few simple procedures frequently called for in both baking and cooking will make any culinary task much less daunting. Skills are gained only through experience, so get out in the kitchen and start practicing! Even the greenest novices should be able to get these basics down pat in no time.

Toasting Nuts and Seeds

Many cooks recommend toasting nuts and seeds in the oven, but this isn't my method of choice. For one, why heat up the whole kitchen when you don't neccssarily need the oven for the rest of your recipe? Secondly, I don't like the fact that I can't really watch over them or stir when necessary, which leads to horrifically blackened nuts far more often than I'd like to admit. Spare yourself the smoke and drama; try toasting over the stove instead.

Set a medium-sized skillet over moderate heat and toss in your nuts or seeds. Toast only 1–2 cups at a time so that they can all have equal time getting direct heat, thus cooking more evenly. It may start slowly, but once you start smelling that nutty aroma, things move quickly, so don't walk away from this process. Stir every minute or two, until the nuts or seeds are golden brown and highly aromatic. This will take anywhere from 7–15 minutes, depending on your particular variety. Immediately pour the contents of your skillet out onto a plate, to prevent them from continuing to cook and subsequently burn.

Using Whole Vanilla Beans

There may be some killer vanilla extracts on the market these days, but there's still no liquid elixir that can touch the potent, sweet essence of a whole vanilla bean. You want to seek out plump, supple beans that bend easily without snapping. They should have a strong scent that carries a natural sweetness with it. Using them in your recipes is simple: Slit one bean lengthwise with a sharp knife and scrape out the tiny seeds within. Add those seeds to your mixture, and be thorough to extract every bit of bean you can.

For additional flavor, toss the spent vanilla bean pods into an ice cream base as well, to infuse, and then remove before churning. Personally, I prefer to save the pods instead in a container of granulated sugar to create incredible vanilla sugar, which does wonders as the crust of crème brûlée.

Grinding Whole Spices

Ready-to-use, ground spices have their place and work quite well in most cases, but if you would just try grinding them from whole seeds to taste the difference, it may be hard to go back.

Using the same technique as you would to toast nuts over the stove top, toast your whole spices first. This will bring out the aromatic and flavorful oils, allowing them to have a stronger and fuller taste. Just keep a very close eye on them, as they tend to toast very quickly; about 5–8 minutes should do it. They may not appear any different in color, but don't worry, you will definitely smell the difference. Let the spices cool completely before grinding down to a fine powder in a spice or coffee grinder. To achieve the finest consistency, you may want to first try freezing the spices. Measure out for your recipes only after completely ground, as whole spices would measure out to very different amounts, compared to powdered.

Thickening a Custard

If I had a penny for every time I had a cauldron of bubbling nondairy milk boil over and redecorate the kitchen . . . Well, I think you know how the rest of that goes. It's not at all hard to thicken ice cream bases, custards, or puddings, but the key is that you must give it your undivided attention. Whisk vigorously before turning on the heat to break up any possible clumps hidden anywhere within the mixture, and then make sure that you never venture above medium heat. Medium-low is a better bet for the easily distracted, just as an extra measure of insurance. Whisk occasionally at first, every few minutes, to ensure that nothing is sticking to or burning at the bottom of the pot. As bubbles begin to form around the edges, keep stirring constantly, with one hand hovering above the heat control. A rapid boil can quickly overflow the confines of any pot, so as soon as it's reached that stage, immediately kill the heat and move the whole pot off the burner. Keep whisking for a minute longer, to help facilitate the cooling process and ensure that no lumps form right at the end.

Straining Custards and Sauces

Lumps happen, and that's a fact of life. They *don't* have to ruin your desserts, though! For the smoothest results possible, it's a good idea to strain every single thickened liquid before allowing it to cool or further set, to remove possible starchy clumps. Use a fine-mesh sieve to filter out any offending particles, and try not to press the contents through with your spatula. Rather, tap on the side of the strainer firmly and rapidly to help gravity carry the mixture through. Some bases are simply too thick to strain without a bit of additional pressure, though, so don't be afraid to get a spatula in there if you need to. Discard any lumps you may catch.

Storing Desserts in the Freezer

Air is the biggest enemy of food preservation, so the key to proper storage is investing in sturdy, airtight containers. BPA-free plastic is your best bet, since it has more flexibility, and can more easily withstand the rigors of freezing and thawing. Glass containers may be pretty and easier to see into, but they become exceedingly apt to break once frozen, and it really bites when you get shards of glass in your dessert. In the case of ice cream or frosting, if there's a lot of empty headroom in the container after filling it, place a piece of parchment or wax paper directly on the surface before closing up the container, to help stave off freezer burn.

For cakes, wrap layers separately in plastic wrap, and let frosting thaw completely before whipping back into shape with your stand mixer and applying; do *not* microwave because it will simply turn into a buttery puddle of sugar.

Cookies and cupcakes can be wrapped individually to thaw as cravings strike, or bundled in containers, separated by layers of wax paper.

Fruit desserts, like crisps, crumbles, and especially pies, do not keep well in the fridge let alone the freezer, and should be eaten as soon as possible. If you're worried about leftovers, make smaller batches and bake in single servings.

Don't forget, the freezer doesn't cryogenically preserve foods, and even the most carefully packed edibles don't last forever. Be sure to label all containers with titles and dates either on stickers or pieces of masking tape, and keep frozen treats for no more than a maximum of four months (although that's never been much of a concern in my household, at least).

Rolling Out Pie Dough

Warmth is the mortal enemy of pie dough, so always keep your crusts chilled. That means you should leave them in the fridge until the very last minute, handle them as little as possible, and keep them on the counter only as long as they need to be there. As the dough warms up, the margarine begins to melt, so the dough will become stickier and thus harder to work with, not to mention the fact that you will lose flakiness in the final baked crust. From the moment it hits your lightly floured counter, it should get your full attention. Turn the disk over in the flour to coat both sides, so that it doesn't stick to either the counter or your rolling pin. You can add a pinch of additional flour to the top if it seems to cling at any point.

Start in the center of the disk and apply firm but gentle pressure outward with your rolling pin, smoothing out the dough as evenly as you can. Roll a few times in one direction, gently lift and turn the dough, and roll again in a new direction. It's easiest if you can stand at a corner, so you can change position more and move the dough around less. Don't worry that it's not a perfect circle (it never will be, even after you've made a million pies). Focus on thickness; even thickness is the key to even baking. An eighth of an inch is the magic width that works best to support a filling without burning to a crisp or remaining doughy, so use a ruler or just pretend you're making thin cookies to approximate the measurement.

Some people prefer to roll out dough between two pieces of parchment paper or silicone baking mats to get around the use of flour, thus preventing possible messes. I'm not a big fan of this method, since my crusts still stuck to the paper and are more likely to tear upon removal, but this method may be more effective in colder climates.

Transferring Dough to a Pie Pan

So you've got your thin round of dough, ready to use. Now what? It's time to maneuver it into your vessel of choice, a 9-inch round standard pie pan unless otherwise specified in the particular recipe you're making. Since the shape of the crust is rather unwieldy as it stands, I like to make mine more compact for an easy transfer. Very gently fold the whole round in half, without pressing down on the seam or sides, and then fold it in half again in the same fashion, so that it's ultimately a quarter of its former size. Lift the folded round from underneath, handling it lightly, and place the folded point right in the center of your pan. Fully unfold it to fill the dish, easing it up the sides and pressing any creases flat again. You should have more or less even amounts of excess dough overhanging the edges if you've situated it correctly.

Fluting or Crimping the Crust

Neaten up the edges before attempting anything fancy, so that you have the same amount of material to work with all the way around. Use kitchen shears or a very sharp knife to trim the excess dough to about ½ inch away from the rim of the pan. For a single crust, lift up that edge and fold it underneath itself, so that it's resting on the lip of the pie pan and the cut edge is hidden. Continue folding all the way around, straightening and smoothing as you go. The simplest crimp is made with the tines of a fork; just press the fork into the rim again and again until the lines match up in the place where you began. My favorite sort of crimp is done with just three fingers; use two fingers on one hand to press the interior side of the lip, and one finger on the other to press the opposite side of the crust in the center of those two fingers. Repeat all the way around to form a tight scalloped design. For a larger, loopy scallop, turn that single finger into a hook and press that into the side of the crust, using your opposite hands to indent the larger space on either side of the "U" shape.

Making Decorative Crusts and Cutouts

If you should find yourself with leftover scraps of dough, don't throw them away—you can use them to make fancy decorations on top of your pie! Just use any small, simple-shaped cookie cutters to punch out your pieces. Adhere them to either the exposed rim of a single crust or the top of a double crust in exactly the same way:

Use a lightly moistened finger to dampen the back of your shape before firmly pressing it into place. If you want to decorate the entire border of the pie, this method can take the place of a traditional crimped edge.

Creating the Perfect Golden-Brown Finish

All it takes for any food to cook to a mouthwatering shade of amber is a bit of heat and either sugar or protein. Protein enables the Maillard reaction, whereas sugars create caramelization. Either way, it all leads to one conclusion: Delicious, beautiful food. In the case of pastries, the dough naturally contains a bit of each macronutrient, which allows browning in the oven without further intervention. If you want to enhance that reaction, and potentially add a touch of shine, that's where a swipe of *Golden Pastry Glaze* comes in handy.

1 teaspoon arrowroot powder
1 teaspoon light corn syrup
3 tablespoons water

Whisk ingredients together vigorously, to dissolve the arrowroot smoothly into the liquid. Use a pastry brush, basting brush, or large art brush that has never been used with paint to apply the glaze to the upper crust or exposed edges of a single crust. Bake as per usual.

Alternately, plain nondairy milk can also give you good results; soy milk is best in this case, since it's the highest in protein.

Catching Drips in the Oven

Pies, and fruit pies especially, are notorious for bubbling up and over the confines of their pans. Those dastardly sticky fillings seem hellbent on making their mark all over your clean oven. Don't let the pie win this fight! Although spillover can't be controlled, it can be contained. Every time you bake a pie, no matter how clean and dry it may appear, always place a large, rimmed baking sheet on the oven rack directly below it. This will catch any drips thrown overboard, and though it won't prevent them from burning during the baking process, it will save you the hassle of scrubbing out the oven later. It's much easier to clean a single baking sheet than a whole cavernous oven.

Substituting Frozen Fruit for Fresh

Cravings don't always follow the seasons, so the temptation to sneak in a blueberry pie in the middle of a January blizzard is completely understandable. While it is possible to use frozen fruits where fresh are called for, bear in mind that a pie is only as good as its ingredients, and nothing can compare to the flavor of ripe produce at the height of its growing season. There is also no direct conversion from fresh to frozen, since the freezing process creates many ice crystals inside the fruit which extract additional water when thawed. To prevent your pies from becoming a soupy mess, you must first fully thaw and drain the fruit. Only then can you measure and use it, although the weight will be different thanks to the water that was removed, so your best bet is to stick with volume measures. Otherwise, weigh out how much liquid you're removing once the fruit has thawed, and add in that same measurement of whole, thawed fruit to equal the same final weight called for in the recipe.

Caramelizing Crème Brûlée

After preparing and chilling the crème in question, use a paper towel to dab off any condensation or moisture that may have formed on the surface of the custard. Sprinkle sugar generously over the top, tilting the ramekin around so that the entire area is evenly covered; tap off any excess that doesn't stick.

If using a kitchen torch, start by holding the flame 3–4 inches away from the sugar, continuously moving the torch in a gentle circular motion. If you allow it to rest in one area for too long, you'll get uneven browning or worse, burning, so pay close attention to the flame. Slowly move in closer, until you start to see the granules liquefy. Keep on moving, turning the ramekin to reach all areas of the top, until all of the sugar has dissolved and turned a golden amber brown.

If brûléeing in the oven, position the oven rack at the very highest spot in the oven and turn on the broiler to high. When hot, place the ramekins directly under the broiler and let cook for 5–10 minutes, until the sugar has dissolved and is bubbling away. Rotate frequently to allow even browning.

Let the caramelized sugar rest for at least 5 minutes before serving, for it to set up to a hard crack. Completed crème brûlée can be stored in the refrigerator for no more than 30 minutes before the caramel begins to melt.

Making Vanilla Sugar

How can you improve upon an already stellar dessert? Vanilla sugar is the magic ingredient capable of turning the flavor up to 11. It makes the biggest difference in more delicately seasoned or simpler sweets where the addition is more detectable, but it adds a subtle something extra to anything it graces. Try it on top of crème brûlée, to sweeten whipped cream, or even in hot drinks, for starters. To make a practically unlimited supply, fill a jar of any size with standard granulated sugar. Every time you use a vanilla bean, jam the spent, dry pods right in the center. Over time, the vanilla will infuse its essence throughout the sugar, becoming stronger with age. Continue replenishing both the beans and sugar periodically, and you will always be prepared with some on hand.

Troubleshooting

Cake or bread didn't rise?

Since there are no eggs to provide leavening in vegan baking, cakes rely entirely on chemical leaveners, such as baking powder and soda. If you mismeasure these critical ingredients, there will be dire consequences, so be diligent and stick to the recipe as written! Tweaking flavors and playing around to put your own spin on things is encouraged, but altering the basic structure is not recommended.

Also, be certain to check that both baking powder and soda are in good working condition. Those little boxes tend to stick around forever, and if you don't do a whole lot of baking, chance are they've gone bad and lost their leavening ability. To test the efficacy of baking powder, place 1 teaspoon into a small dish, and mix in ½ teaspoon water. For baking soda, you want to combine 1 teaspoon with ½ teaspoon of vinegar. In both cases, they should bubble up right away, or else it's time to replace them.

Yeast is a living organism (but not an animal or animal product; they're technically classified in the kingdom Fungi, just like mushrooms) so it makes good sense that at some point they "die" and cease to function properly. Dried in packets, they're in a dormant state, and must be reawakened before being baked. That's why most recipes recommend proofing, that is, soaking the yeast in warm water, before adding it into the dough. If after 5–10 minutes, it doesn't become frothy, your yeast is a goner. I like to store my yeast in the fridge, and I've thus far never had any expire on me.

Tough, dry cake or muffin?

Sounds like a gluten problem. Gluten develops when you beat or mix a wheat-based mixture too much, making it stretchy as if you were making bread dough. Unfortunately, this is not what you want for cakes. Instead of a tender crumb, that extra gluten will give you a tight, unpleasantly chewy baked good. A side effect of having more gluten in the cake is that it will also tend to squeeze out or absorb more liquid, leaving the baked good in question with a drier interior. If you're ever unsure of how much to mix, just assume that for cakes, less is better.

Dry, hard, or crumbly cookies?

The secret to cravably soft, chewy cookies is hardly a secret at all, but common sense when it comes right down to it. Bake your cookies for less time, and allow them to sit on the hot baking sheet longer to finish cooking at a slower, gentler pace. When I pull mine out of the oven, they tend to look like they're not quite done, and perhaps even still raw in the center. It depends on the exact cookie and with practice, you'll get a better feel for when exactly to take them out, but always start by baking them for the lesser amount of time suggested in a recipe. For example, if the recipe recommends 8–12 minutes, start by baking them for only 8, and check your results. If worse comes to worst, underbaked cookies can always take a second round in the oven.

Cake or bread gooey in the center?

This is quite possibly one of the most common baking problems I hear about, which is such a shame because it's very easily prevented. It's an issue of simply not baking the item in question for long enough, even though it may look browned to perfection on the outside. Always be sure to check the interior by inserting a toothpick or wooden skewer into the center, all the way down to the bottom. This method does have its pitfalls though, should there be chocolate chips that give the false impression that your cake is still raw in the middle, so you may wish to poke in multiple places. Bear in mind that the holes will show, so unless you're covering the top with frosting, this may not be the best idea!

If you repeatedly end up with cakes that are done on the outside but raw in the center, double-check your oven temperature—it's likely that it's running hot. You can compensate by dialing a slightly lower temperature than is recommended in the recipe, or by tenting a pieces of aluminum foil over your baked goods in the final minutes of baking, to ensure that the tops don't burn or become overdone.

Cake domed in the center?

Don't panic—this is a common problem with a very simple solution. The easiest way to correct a cosmetic defect like this is to wait until the cake is completely cool, and then take a long, serrated knife, and slice off the hump. Voilà, a perfectly flat cake, and a little snack for the baker! If you're worried about crumbs or want to avoid such a situation altogether, try lowering your oven temperature by about 25 degrees. It's possible that your oven might be running a bit hotter than anticipated, causing that edible mountain to form in the first place. Double-check next time by placing an additional thermometer inside the oven, and compare the readings to the external display.

Flat muffins with no tops?

Exactly the opposite of the problem described directly above, in this case, you might want to consider raising the oven temperature 25 degrees. Additionally, make sure your batter isn't too runny; it should definitely be thicker than cupcake batter. Don't be shy when you fill the tins, because unlike cupcakes, you want to mound these up right to the top, and possibly even over. Make sure you do pile on the batter right in the center, to encourage those golden-brown peaks to form.

Cupcakes remove their own papers?

Yes, nudist cupcakes. Some people never experience this phenomenon, and I hadn't until very recently when baking a large batch (16 dozen) cupcakes for a massive order at work. All was going according to plan, little cakes marching out of the oven left and right . . . but then while they sat on the counter cooling, they began to spontaneously undress. After having this happen a couple times on giant batches, I've come to find that there are two issues that could be the culprit here; Most likely, the cupcakes are placed too close together while cooling, thus "steaming" each other and causing too much moisture to form between the cake and wrapper. Being paper, it doesn't take much for the wrapper to give up the fight and fall off.

Secondly, it's possible that there is too much oil in the cakes. That was my main problem, because although I scaled up the recipe, I simply multiplied most of the amounts. It's not a straight conversion when you get into such large scale baking. I've been cutting back on the oil for batches of more than 4 dozen, and my cupcakes have stayed properly dressed ever since.

Cupcakes won't come out of their papers?

Unfortunately, the only thing that can be done about this problem is to buy different cupcake papers next time. Most manufacturers use paper that is at least somewhat waterproof, and some of the higher quality options are even laminated or coated in food-grade silicone, like a non-stick pan, to make for easier cupcake removal. However, the cheapest options are unlikely to offer any easy-release guarantees, and if you find that your cakes keep getting trapped in their wrappers time and again, you may want to start looking into other brands.

Ice cream too hard or not creamy?

Ice cream can be a tricky dessert to make, simply because the texture is largely dependent on the machine that you use to churn it in. If the machine churns too slowly, it will cause larger ice crystals to form, thus giving you an icier finished dessert. Additionally, if it doesn't mix in much air—which is what gives the ice cream greater volume (often called "overrun" in ice cream–speak)—then it will ultimately freeze with a much denser consistency, which can translate into hard ice cream.

Another thing you may want to check is what temperature your freezer is. The average freezer runs at around 0°F. If yours clocks in far below that, you'll undoubtedly get more solidly frozen ice cream straight from the chill chest. Finally, bear in mind that the longer your ice cream sits in the freezer, the harder and also drier it will become. Yes, ice cream *can* go bad and become freezer-burnt if you stash it for over 4 months or so . . . Although I must admit, I've never found that to be a problem in this household.

The best solution for almost all of these problems is to simply remove your ice cream from the freezer 10–15 minutes before you want to serve it. This will allow it to soften slightly, become easier to scoop, and reach a temperature where the flavors will be more pronounced (since our taste buds can't detect flavors as well when foods are colder). If you're in a rush, you can also microwave it for bursts of 5 seconds at a time, until soft enough to scoop, but not melted.

Frosting not light and fluffy?

Patience, grasshopper! Although the frosting may be smooth and creamy after just a minute of whipping, it takes much more time for it to take in enough air to become lighter in texture. Give it a solid 5–10 minutes before panicking, and if that doesn't do it, you may want to add a teaspoon or two of water if it seems too thick, or ¼–½ cup more confectioners' sugar if you think it might be too thin. Make sure that you have the whisk attachment installed in your stand mixer, and crank it up to high.

Baked goods didn't turn "golden brown"?

Browning is another form of caramelization, and for caramelization to occur, you must have sugars and heat present. Since the recipes in this cookbook all have some form of sugar and of course, baked goods go into the oven, the problem probably lies in a mismeasurement, erring on the side of too little sugar. Otherwise, your sweets were simply not baked for long enough time.

Chips, nuts, and berries all sank to the bottom?

All of these goodies tend to be much heavier than the batter of most cakes or bar cookies, so it's a simple matter of gravity taking over when you find them all clumped at the bottom. However, by coating the mix-ins evenly in flour before adding the wet ingredients in, you stand a fighting chance of keeping them distributed throughout. If they still fall and this bothers you, you can instead try sprinkling them on top of the batter once spread in the pan, so that they may ultimately end up in the middle as intended.

SWEET STARTS

Loaf it or Leave It: While I love the grab-and-go convenience of individual muffins, it's a snap to convert this recipe into loaf format for superlative banana bread. Simply pour the batter into a lightly greased 8x4-inch loaf pan. You may wish to double the topping for fuller coverage, and sprinkle it evenly all over the batter, before placing the loaf pan into the oven. Bake at 350°F (175°C) for 45 to 55 minutes, until a toothpick inserted into the center of the loaf comes out clean.

Better Banana Nut Muffins

Makes 10 to 12 muffins

For the times when each grocery run adds a few extra bananas to the counter, turning the cache into a steadily growing pile of rapidly browning time bombs, every baker needs a reliable banana muffin recipe in their repertoire. Most merely call for one or two mashed bananas, but double down on the fruity flavor with chewy, almost candy-like concentrated natural sweetness of rehydrated dried bananas. These aren't those fried, starchy banana chips you get in the snack aisle. These are actual dried bananas that you can buy or make yourself. If you choose to make them, cut ripe bananas into ¼-inch coins and either dehydrate or bake at the lowest setting on your oven for 3–6 hours, until darkened, dry to the touch, and still slightly flexible. Be sure to make plenty of extra while you're at it, since the plain dried fruit makes for an irresistible snack as is.

BANANA MUFFINS:

1 cup dried banana slices
1 cup water
½ cup unsweetened nondairy milk
½ teaspoon apple cider vinegar
¼ cup olive oil
¼ cup dark brown sugar, firmly
   packed
½ teaspoon vanilla extract
1 cup all-purpose flour
½ cup old-fashioned rolled oats
1 teaspoon baking powder
½ teaspoon baking soda
¼ teaspoon salt
½ teaspoon ground cinnamon
⅛ teaspoon ground nutmeg
2 large, very ripe bananas, mashed
½ cup toasted, chopped pecans

OAT TOPPING:

2 tablespoons turbinado sugar
2 tablespoons old-fashioned
   rolled oats
¼ teaspoon ground cinnamon

Preheat your oven to 375°F (190°C) and lightly grease a set of standard muffin tins.

In a small saucepan, combine the dried bananas with about 1 cup of water. Simmer for around 10 minutes to soften, then remove from the heat, and drain off any excess liquid. Once the banana slices are cool enough to handle, roughly chop them into small pieces about the size of raisins. Set aside.

Combine the nondairy milk and vinegar in a large bowl and let sit for a few minutes before whisking vigorously until frothy. Drizzle in the oil to emulsify, following with the brown sugar and vanilla. Mix until fully incorporated. In a separate bowl, combine the flour, oats, baking powder, baking soda, salt, cinnamon, and nutmeg. Slowly incorporate this dry mixture into the wet, being careful not to overmix. It's fine to leave a few lumps in the batter rather than risk ending up with tough muffins.

Fold in the mashed bananas, pecans, and rehydrated bananas. Distribute the batter evenly into your prepared muffin tins, mounding it toward the center so that it peeks just above the edge of the pan.

For the topping, combine the sugar, oats, and cinnamon. Sprinkle it over the raw batter before placing the pan into the oven. Bake for 14 to 18 minutes, until a toothpick inserted into the center of a muffin comes out clean. Let the muffins rest in the pan for at least 5 minutes before removing them to finish cooling on a wire rack.

Carrot Cake Quinoa Cereal

Makes about 3 cups; 3 to 5 servings

Perhaps I've strayed too far off the pastry path for some, but believe it or not, this quinoa concoction really does satisfy that sweet-tooth craving. Think carrot cake with a crunch, this simple cereal is more like granola in texture, while remaining a bit lighter and perfectly crisp all the way through. Pair with vegan yogurt to evoke the sweetness and gentle twang of cream cheese frosting, and you won't miss the layers one bit. I do fully endorse eating cake for breakfast, no matter what form it takes.

1 cup uncooked quinoa

2 cups carrot juice

¼ cup chopped walnuts (optional)

1 tablespoon flaxseeds, ground

1 tablespoon chia seeds

1 tablespoon olive oil

¼ cup maple syrup

½ teaspoon vanilla extract

1¼ teaspoons ground cinnamon

½ teaspoon ground ginger

¼ teaspoon ground nutmeg

⅛ teaspoon salt

¼ cup chopped dried pineapple

¼ cup raisins

Begin by cooking your quinoa in the carrot juice. Simply bring the carrot juice to a boil in a small pot and add the dry quinoa. Cover, reduce the heat to low, and cook gently for 15 to 20 minutes, until all the liquid has been absorbed. Let cool completely before proceeding. You can speed this up by transferring the cooked quinoa to a large bowl and stirring it around a bit, to release the steam and let it air-dry more quickly.

Preheat your oven to 375°F (190°C) and line a baking sheet with parchment paper or a silicone baking mat.

In a medium bowl, mix the cooled quinoa in with all remaining ingredients except for the dried fruits. Spread the mixture out on your prepared sheet, in as thin and even a layer as you can manage. This will help the cereal bake up nice and crispy, so take your time smoothing it out with either a spatula or lightly moistened hands.

Bake for 45 to 60 minutes, stirring every 15 minutes or so, until lightly browned and dry to the touch. It may still have a little bit of softness and give to it, but don't worry; it will continue to crisp up as it cools.

Let cool completely before tossing in the pineapple and raisins. Store in an airtight container for up to a week at room temperature.

Chocolate-Glazed Peanut Butter Scones

Makes 4 scones

Competition is fierce these days, with every nut and seed vying for top honors, but I still believe that peanut butter may just be the world's most perfect spread. Crunchy or creamy, spiced or salted, there's always at least two or three jars of the stuff taking up residence in my pantry. This nutty wonder works its way into countless recipes since it's such a reliably satisfying staple. More than just a toast topper, peanut butter plays the key role in creating the flaky structure of these scones, coincidentally reducing the amount of fat typically found lacquering this buttery breakfast treat. Naturally, this logic justifies the more hedonistic chocolate glaze drizzled over the top.

PEANUT BUTTER SCONES:

1½ cups all-purpose flour
2 tablespoons granulated sugar
2 teaspoons baking powder
¼ teaspoon salt
2 tablespoons vegan butter
¼ cup crunchy peanut butter
1 teaspoon vanilla extract
½ cup unsweetened nondairy milk

CHOCOLATE PEANUT BUTTER GLAZE:

⅓ cup confectioners' sugar
1 tablespoon Dutch-process cocoa powder
1 tablespoon creamy peanut butter
1 tablespoon unsweetened nondairy milk

Preheat your oven to 400ºF (205ºC) and line a baking sheet with a silicone baking mat or parchment paper.

In a medium bowl, combine the flour, sugar, baking powder, and salt. Cut the butter into small pieces and use a fork or a pastry cutter to break it up, along with the crunchy peanut butter, into the flour mixture. Continue cutting the fats into the mixture until it resembles large, coarse crumbs, at which point you can stir in the vanilla. Slowly drizzle in the nondairy milk, one tablespoon at a time, stirring just until the dough starts to come together into a ball. Try not to work the dough any more than necessary.

Drop all the dough onto your silicone baking mat and shape it into a rough circle about 1½-inches thick. This is a rather sticky dough, but work with it gently and it should cooperate. Lightly moisten or grease your hands to help manage the tacky texture, if needed. Cut the circle into 4 quarters with a very sharp knife or bench scraper, so each piece looks somewhat triangular, and separate them on the baking sheet so that each has room to cook. Bake for 15 to 20 minutes, until they turn lightly golden brown. Cool your scones on the baking sheet for at least 5 minutes before transferring to a cooling rack.

For the glaze, combine the confectioners' sugar, cocoa powder, creamy peanut butter, and nondairy milk together in a small bowl. Mix thoroughly until smooth, and drizzle over the cooled scones.

Figgy Graham Scones

Makes 4 to 6 scones

Before graham flour ever turned into crackers and became inseparable from the simple childhood snack, it was already making waves as a wholesome, flavorful foundation in many humble confections. Subtly nutty, pleasantly sandy in texture, it's these unique qualities that place these unassuming scones in a category all their own. Flecked with sultry, chewy chunks of luscious dried figs, prepare the scones in advance and set yourself up for success come breakfast time. Try them lightly toasted with a schmear of vegan cream cheese and jam, or a pat of vegan butter slowly melting over the top, for an exceptionally delicious wake-up call.

1 cup graham flour
½ cup whole wheat pastry flour
⅓ cup granulated sugar
2 teaspoons baking powder
¼ teaspoon salt
¼ teaspoon ground cinnamon
¼ cup vegan butter
¾ cups chopped dried figs
1 teaspoon vanilla extract
4–6 tablespoons unsweetened
   nondairy milk

Preheat your oven to 375ºF (190ºC) and line a baking sheet with a silicone baking mat or parchment paper.

In a medium bowl, combine the flours, sugar, baking powder, salt, and cinnamon. Cut the butter into small pieces and use your fingers or a pastry cutter to press it into the flour mixture. Continue coating as many grains as possible until you create a coarse, pebble-like consistency. Stir in the figs and vanilla. Add the nondairy milk, one tablespoon at a time, until the mixture just comes together as cohesive dough. The amount will depend on your humidity level, so don't be afraid to use more or less, if necessary.

Turn the dough out of the bowl, and firmly press it into a circle that is about one inch tall. Cut your circle into even quarters or sixths, depending on your appetite, and carefully move the divided dough onto your prepared baking sheet. Bake for 14 to 16 minutes, until the scones just begin to brown around the edges. Let cool on the sheet, and serve either warm or at room temperature.

Fruited Focaccia

Makes 16 servings

Italians would be up in arms over this shamelessly inauthentic rendition of their beloved flatbread. Focaccia is supposed to be savory bread of the utmost simplicity, lavished with olive oil, dotted with herbs, maybe sun-dried tomatoes, or perhaps a few briny olives at the most. There's good reason why the classic take remains a timeless dinnertime side dish, but why let tradition limit your creativity? Enriched with plump dried fruits and a hint of bright citrus, this sweet twist on the usual yeast bread turns it into a tasty morsel to help jump-start your day. Any other combination of fruity additions could work well, so use your favorites if you aren't keen on these recommendations.

3 cups water (reserve 1 cup after soaking)

1 cup raisins

½ cup dried cranberries

½ cup chopped dried apricots

½ cup chopped dried pineapple

½ cup chopped dried apples

1 cup orange juice

¼ cup olive oil

2¼ teaspoons (¼-ounce) packet active dry yeast

5–6 cups all-purpose flour

½ cup granulated sugar, divided

1 teaspoon salt

Bring the water to a boil in a large pot and turn off the heat. Add in the dried fruit and let it soak for about 15 minutes to rehydrate. Drain the fruit but save 1 cup of the excess liquid. In a medium bowl, mix the reserved soaking liquid with the orange juice, oil, and yeast. Set aside.

Into a large bowl, toss the rehydrated fruit along with 2 cups of flour, ¼ cup of sugar, and the salt. Add in about half of your liquid ingredients and mix thoroughly until you achieve a smooth dough. Add in another 2 cups of flour along with the remainder of the liquid before mixing again. You don't want the dough to be too sticky, so you may need to introduce anywhere from 1 to 2 more cups of flour, depending on the moisture content of your dough. At this point, you will need to work the dough with either a dough hook installed in your stand mixer or with your hands. When fully combined, you should have a cohesive ball of dough that can be easily handled. Continue to knead with the dough hook or by hand on a lightly floured surface for 5 to 10 minutes, until the dough becomes smooth and elastic. Let rest for 10 minutes before proceeding.

Thoroughly grease a 12 x 17-inch jelly-roll pan and drop the dough on top. Use your fingers to poke the dough down at random intervals, cover loosely with a clean kitchen towel, and let the pan sit in a warm place to rise for about an hour. When it appears to have doubled in volume, sprinkle the remaining ¼ cup of sugar evenly over the top, and bake in a 400°F (205°C) oven for 25 to 30 minutes. When it is done, the bread should have a solid crust that is a deep golden brown. Let cool and slice into 3 x 4-inch pieces.

Enjoy this stand-alone breakfast bread as is, or top with your favorite jam for even more fruit flavor.

Golden Glazed Doughnuts

Makes 6 to 8 doughnuts plus 8 or more doughnut holes

Remember those crispy, creamy donuts of yore, rolling down the conveyor belt behind glass windows, hurtling through a curtain of cascading white icing? Nothing can replicate the experience of biting into one of those soft, tender rings, still hot off the line . . . but it's entirely possible to create an even better version in the comfort of your own home. Instead of just melting away to coat your tongue in sugary residue, these beauties possess both substance and sweet nostalgic satisfaction.

DOUGHNUTS:

2¼ teaspoons (¼-ounce) packet
    active dry yeast
2 tablespoons warm water
3 tablespoons vegan butter
¼ cup granulated sugar
1 tablespoon whole flaxseeds
¾ cup unsweetened nondairy milk
1 teaspoon apple cider vinegar
½ teaspoon vanilla extract
½ teaspoon salt
2½ cups all-purpose flour
1 quart canola or vegetable oil,
    for frying

GLAZE:

3 tablespoons vegan butter
1 cup confectioners' sugar
1 teaspoon vanilla extract
1 tablespoon water

TO FINISH:

Rainbow sprinkles (optional)

Sprinkle the yeast over the warm water in a small dish and let sit for 5 minutes, until it reactivates and becomes a bit frothy. Meanwhile, in your stand mixer, fitted with the beater attachment, cream the butter and sugar together and beat until fluffy. Grind the flaxseeds into a fine powder using a spice grinder before adding it into the mixer, followed by the nondairy milk, vinegar, vanilla, and salt. Incorporate the water and yeast next. The mixture will likely look a bit lumpy at this point, so don't stress over appearances. Add in 2 cups of flour, letting the mixer run until it's fully incorporated. Add in the remaining ½ cup of flour and continue mixing to combine.

Replace the beater with a dough hook, if you have one, and agitate the dough on medium speed for about 5 minutes. Alternatively, turn the dough out onto a lightly floured surface and knead it by hand. Continue until it feels smooth and elastic—tacky but not too sticky. Move the dough into a lightly greased bowl, cover, and place in a warm location to rise. Wait for the dough to double in volume before proceeding, approximately 1 hour.

Grease a baking sheet and set aside. On a lightly floured surface, turn the dough out of the bowl and gently roll it out to a thickness of approximately ½-inch. Use a doughnut cutter, or one large and one small circular cookie cutter (about 4 inches and 1 inch, respectively), lightly dipped in flour, to create each doughnut shape. Move the raw doughnuts onto the greased baking sheet. Cut any remaining dough into small circles to make doughnut

(continued on next page)

holes and stash these on the baking sheet as well. Cover loosely with a clean dish towel, and let them rise for another hour or so, until they double in size.

Once the dough is ready, begin heating the oil in a deep fryer or large pot. While the oil is heating, prepare the glaze. Over medium-low heat, melt the butter and whisk in the sugar, vanilla, and water until the glaze is completely smooth. Pour the glaze into a shallow dish that is wide enough to accommodate your donuts. Set aside. Don't worry if the glaze begins to solidify while you are frying. The heat from the donuts will melt it back to a liquid state.

When the oil hits 350ºF (175ºC) you're ready to start frying. First and foremost, be very careful! You will only be cooking one or two donuts at a time, to avoid crowding the pot and ensuring they cook evenly. Gently slide the raw dough into the oil using a wide slotted spatula. Fry for about 2 minutes per side, until deeply golden brown. Remove using the same spatula, briefly pat any excess oil off using a paper towel, and dip them into the glaze while the doughnut is still warm. Top with rainbow sprinkles, if desired. Repeat this process for the remaining doughnuts and doughnut holes.

Chocoholics, Unite! In the battle between chocolate and vanilla, the only clear winner is both. Keep the peace by whipping up a quick chocolate glaze. Simply add ¼ cup Dutch-process cocoa powder to the glaze recipe.

Hearty Granola Waffles

Makes 4 to 6 servings

Plain Jane waffles would spill their syrup with one glance at these crisp, golden brown, deeply cratered beauties. The batter itself is bursting with a diverse range of flavorful mix-ins, colored by whichever unique blend strikes your fancy. Use a Belgian waffle iron to make deeper pockets to accommodate even more granola goodness on top.

3 cups all-purpose flour

1 teaspoon baking powder

½ teaspoon baking soda

½ teaspoon salt

2½ cups unsweetened nondairy milk

¼ cup maple syrup

¼ cup olive oil

2 teaspoons apple cider vinegar

1 teaspoon vanilla extract

1½ cups granola, store-bought or homemade (page 51)

Preheat your waffle iron so it's ready as soon as the batter is prepared. Combine the flour, baking powder, baking soda, and salt in a large bowl. In a separate bowl, whisk together the nondairy milk, maple syrup, oil, vinegar, and vanilla. Pour the wet ingredients into the bowl of dry and stir until just incorporated; it's perfectly fine to leave a few lumps remaining.

Once the waffle iron is hot, lightly grease with cooking spray or olive oil, and ladle the batter on top. The exact amount depends on the size of your waffle iron. Sprinkle about ¼ cup of granola over the raw batter for each waffle before closing the lid.

Cook for 4 to 6 minutes, until evenly golden brown. Serve hot, with additional granola and Whipped Coconut Cream (page 243), if desired. If you'd like to prepare the waffles in advance and save them for later, allow them to cool completely before storing them in an airtight plastic bag or container. The waffles will keep in the fridge for up to a week, or in the freezer for up to two months.

Some people say that the best part of a cinnamon roll is the cream cheese icing, and I must admit, they make a pretty compelling argument. If you can't imagine forgoing that gooey goodness, you can make a **Quick Cream Cheese Icing** by mixing together 4 ounces (½ cup) vegan cream cheese, ½ cup confectioners' sugar, and 2 to 4 tablespoons nondairy milk until smooth. Drizzle to your heart's content!

Oatmeal Raisin Rolls

Makes 12 to 15 rolls

Cinnamon rolls are a delight bright and early in the morning, unless of course you're the baker who had to wake up long before sunrise to make them. You could choose the traditional route, agonizing over long waiting periods while the dough rises . . . or, you could skip straight to the good part and whip up a different sort of swirled bun, without the fuss. These soft and tender spirals come together very quickly and are considerably heartier than your typical breakfast pastry, so you can still feel virtuous for eating well, even if you oversleep.

¾ cup unsweetened non-dairy milk

2¼ teaspoons (¼-ounce) packet rapid rise yeast

¼ cup vegan butter

¼ cup granulated sugar

1 teaspoon vanilla extract

1 tablespoon baking powder

½ teaspoon salt

1¼ cups whole wheat pastry flour

1¼ cups old-fashioned rolled oats

1 cup all-purpose flour

½ cup coconut sugar or dark brown sugar, firmly packed

½ teaspoon ground cinnamon

½ cup raisins

Preheat your oven to 400°F (205°C) and line a baking sheet with a silicone baking mat or parchment paper.

Heat the nondairy milk in a microwave-safe dish for 30 to 60 seconds, or until just warmed through. Add the yeast and let sit until it becomes frothy, about 5 minutes. Meanwhile, in a separate bowl, cream the butter, sugar, and vanilla together. Add in the baking powder, salt, whole wheat pastry flour, and oats, mixing thoroughly to combine. The yeast should have become visibly active by now, so pour the yeast mixture into the batter, mixing thoroughly. Finally, add the all-purpose flour, and stir well, so that everything is completely combined.

Turn the dough out onto a generously floured surface and knead it briefly for about 5 minutes. Press the dough out manually to form a nice even rectangle of about ¼ inch thickness. Exact measurements aren't all that important, but keep in mind that a longer, thinner shape will produce more rolls that are smaller, while a shorter, wider shape will produce fewer rolls that are larger and have more layers. Regardless of what you ultimately end up with, sprinkle the brown sugar and cinnamon evenly over the top, leaving about 1 inch on one of the long sides clear. Sprinkle the raisins over the brown sugar and press them gently into the surface of the dough. Starting at the long side where the sugar goes all the way to the edge, roll the dough carefully without stretching or pulling it. When you get to the edge, very lightly moisten the clean edge of dough with water so that it sticks to the side. Pinch together the edges to seal.

Lay the dough seam-side down on the counter, and gently cut 1-inch pieces with a very sharp knife. Place each roll on your prepared baking sheet, with one of the cut sides down, and bake for 15 to 20 minutes, until they just begin to turn golden brown all over.

Enjoy these rolls plain for breakfast, or top them with icing for a more decadent treat.

Power-Hungry Granola

Makes 4 to 6 servings

Back in the day of early classes and long school days, my go-to breakfast would almost always be some sort of granola. Instant, easy to eat, and delicious, I could pretty much live on nothing but cereal for days on end. Unfortunately, not all granola is created equal, often leading to devastating sugar comas and midday crashes, right when I needed energy most. Now older and wiser, I decided to take matters into my own hands, in search of truly smart fuel. Full of whole grains, protein, good fats, and just enough sweetness to entice the taste buds, this concoction put an end to my midday slumps. Double, or even triple, this recipe to set yourself up for success during your most demanding weeks.

1 cup textured vegetable protein (TVP)

1 cup old-fashioned rolled oats

3 cups puffed quinoa, millet, and/ or brown rice cereal

2 teaspoons ground cinnamon

⅓ cup dark brown sugar, firmly packed

½ teaspoon vanilla extract

¼ cup maple syrup

⅓ cup apple juice

2 tablespoons olive oil

⅓ cup dried cranberries

⅓ cup raisins

½ cup sliced almonds

Preheat your oven to 300°F (150°C) and lightly grease a jelly-roll pan, or any other large baking sheet with a rim or shallow sides.

Stir together the TVP, oats, puffed cereal, and cinnamon in a large bowl. In a separate bowl, combine the sugar and all the liquid ingredients. Pour the liquid mixture over the dry goods, folding it together until all the cereal is completely coated. Spread out in as flat a layer as possible into your prepared pan or dish. Bake for 30 to 35 minutes, stirring at 10-minute intervals so your granola doesn't burn. Let cool completely on the sheet.

Once cool, stir in the cranberries, raisins, and almonds, and serve with your favorite nondairy milk or simply eat right out of your hand. Store any leftover granola in an airtight container, for up to two weeks.

Strawberry Love Muffins

Makes 10 to 12 muffins

Foodies will all agree that the quickest way to a person's heart is through their stomach. Thus, it seems only logical that when Valentine's Day rolls around, something edible must take center stage. While chocolate and candies are obvious considerations, try this romantic treat for healthy departure from such over-the-top indulgence. Of course, regularly shaped muffins work just as well if you lack the necessary equipment, or just want to spread the love all year round. Whatever vessel ends up becoming a home to your blushing batter, these muffins are guaranteed to win hearts.

1½ cups all-purpose flour

½ cup granulated sugar

1 teaspoon baking powder

1 teaspoon baking soda

¼ teaspoon salt

½ cup unsweetened nondairy milk

¼ cup lemon juice

⅓ cup olive oil

1 teaspoon vanilla extract

1 cup fresh or frozen and thawed
   strawberries, sliced

Preheat your oven to 375°F (190°C) and grease 10 to 12 muffin tins, depending on how large you'd like to make them.

Begin by mixing together your dry ingredients (flour through salt) in a large bowl. Gently stir in the nondairy milk, lemon juice, oil, and vanilla, but be careful not to overmix; a few lumps are okay! Fold in the strawberries and pour the batter into your prepared muffin tins, filling them about ¾ of the way to the top. Slide your filled tins into the oven and bake for 15 to 20 minutes, until a toothpick inserted into the center of a muffin comes out clean.

Let the muffins sit for at least 10 minutes before removing them from the pan. Enjoy with someone you love.

Sweet & Simple French Toast

Makes 4 slices

When I first attempted French toast, it was still very early in my "career" as a vegan. Because I had yet to really move into my element in the kitchen, my whole family remained skeptical of what could be done without milk or eggs. Even my mom, the eternal optimist, was not exactly convinced that French toast without the usual animal products would be entirely palatable. Still, I persevered and came up with this creation to share with her. All it took was one mouthful of this delicious dish for my mother to start thinking about veganism in an entirely different way.

4 (1-inch thick) slices ciabatta
  or French bread
2 tablespoons whole wheat flour
1 teaspoon nutritional yeast
2 tablespoons dark brown sugar
¼ teaspoon kala namak,
  or plain salt
½ teaspoon ground cinnamon
⅛ teaspoon ground nutmeg
1 cup unsweetened nondairy milk
1 cup crushed corn flake cereal
2–4 teaspoons olive oil or
  vegan butter

Begin by lightly toasting your bread, allowing it to become a bit firmer, which will make it more receptive to the extra moisture you will be adding.

Combine the dry ingredients (not including cereal) in a shallow pan and make sure they are evenly distributed. Stir in the non-dairy milk and allow it to sit for a minute. Whisk again before using, to ensure that no lumps are left behind. Meanwhile, place the crushed cornflakes in a separate shallow dish and begin heating a large skillet over medium heat. Grease the pan lightly with a drizzle of olive oil or a dab of vegan butter.

Place two slices of bread in the liquid mix at a time, allowing about 1 minute for it to start soaking into the slices. Flip your bread over and let the wet mixture absorb into the other side for another minute. Once saturated but not soggy, carefully lift the slices out with a large spatula and place them into the dish of crushed cornflakes. Lightly press to adhere the coating, flipping to encrust the other side, and finally move them into the hot skillet. Cook for 3 to 5 minutes per side, resisting the urge to push them around or constantly check on the progress to get the best sear. Flip once, and only once.

Once nicely browned and crisp on the outside, transfer the toast to a plate, and repeat the process with the two remaining bread slices. Serve with maple syrup, fruit spread, confectioners' sugar, or any favorite toppings you like.

Zesty Cranberry Crumb Muffins

Makes 12 muffins

Streusel just makes everything better, doesn't it? While these muffins are incredibly good on their own, the crumbly topping bumps them up that extra notch to irresistible. Tangy, tart, and sweet all at the same time, the flavors and textures work in perfect harmony. While perfectly respectable as a grab-and-go breakfast, such sweet little morsels excel as an afternoon snack as well.

CRANBERRY MUFFINS:

¾ cup dried cranberries
¾ cup orange juice
½ cup unsweetened nondairy milk
1 teaspoon apple cider vinegar
⅓ cup olive oil
⅔ cup granulated sugar
1 cup all-purpose flour
½ cup whole wheat pastry flour
1½ teaspoons baking powder
½ teaspoon baking soda
3 tablespoons unsweetened
    applesauce
2 tablespoons orange zest

CRUMB TOPPING:

3 tablespoons vegan butter
⅓ cup all-purpose flour
⅓ cup granulated sugar

Preheat your oven to 375ºF (190ºC) and lightly grease one dozen muffin tins.

Combine the cranberries and orange juice in a saucepan and simmer over medium-low heat for about 10 minutes, until the fruit has absorbed all the liquid. Remove from the heat and let cool.

Combine the nondairy milk and vinegar, whisking vigorously until frothy. Incorporate the oil into the milk mixture and beat until fully emulsified. Add the sugar and mix well. Add in the flours, baking powder, baking soda, and applesauce, being careful not to overmix. Gently fold in the rehydrated cranberries and zest. Spoon the batter into your prepared muffin tins.

For the crumb topping, combine the butter, flour, and sugar with a pastry cutter or fork, until it resembles coarse crumbs. Sprinkle evenly over each mound of raw batter. Bake for 14 to 18 minutes, until a toothpick inserted into the center of a muffin comes out clean. Let the muffins sit for at least 10 minutes before removing them from the pan.

COOKIES & BARS

Almond Avalanche Bars

Makes 24 to 36 bars

Prepare yourself for an almond onslaught! Almonds are all the rage for health nuts and gourmets alike, due to their high levels of antioxidants, unsaturated fats, and most important to me, great taste. If you happen to be a fellow almond fanatic who simply can't get enough, then this bar was made for you. Composed almost entirely of nothing but nuts, even a small square will flood your senses and bowl you over with pure almond satisfaction.

ALMOND CRUST:
½ cup vegan butter
½ cup coconut sugar or dark brown sugar, firmly packed
1⅔ cups almond meal
½ teaspoon salt

ALMOND TOPPING:
2 cups crunchy almond butter
1 cup maple syrup
2 teaspoons vanilla extract
1 cup bittersweet or semisweet chocolate chips (optional)
1 cup sliced almonds

> **Go Nuts!** No matter how bare the pantry gets, I will always have a jar of peanut butter on hand, ready to quell those midnight cravings. Many times it's saved the day for last-minute dessert demands, too. Swap out the almond butter for an equal amount of peanut butter (or hazelnut butter, pecan butter, pistachio butter, cashew butter—you name it) for a delicious departure from the original recipe.

Preheat your oven to 350°F (175°C) and line a 9x13-inch baking pan with aluminum foil. Lightly grease and set aside.

In a medium bowl, cream together the butter and sugar until homogeneous. Slowly incorporate the almond meal, followed by the salt. Transfer the mixture into your prepared baking pan and pat the dough into the bottom, keeping it as even as possible. Bake for 15 to 18 minutes, until firm and lightly browned. Let cool but leave the oven on.

For the topping, mix together the almond butter, maple syrup, and vanilla in a large bowl. Mix until smooth and fully combined but don't go too crazy, as it will continue to thicken the more you mix, which can make it difficult to spread smoothly into the pan. Fold in the chocolate chips, if using (and I do recommend using). Drop this mixture evenly over your crust, pressing and gently spreading as necessary to form an even layer, taking care not to disturb the bottom layer. Sprinkle the sliced almonds over the top and bake for 12 to 15 more minutes. You are not looking for a dry exterior, so it is okay if the bars look moist or underbaked. A raw cookie dough appearance *is* what you are going for.

Let cool *completely* before cutting into bars. By completely, I don't mean cool to the touch. The bars must be cool enough for the chocolate chips to resolidify. If you are not patient, you may end up with a fudgy almond mess! Chill for 1 to 2 hours in advance for the best results.

Apricot Biscotti

Makes approximately 24 biscotti

For such a humble name, these café-inspired treats boast an impressive array of complex flavors. While they are made with vastly different ingredients and techniques than your typical biscotti, the careful attention to each individual component really does produce superior results. These biscotti are suitable for the gluten intolerant, yet the overall taste is so spot-on that they would be right at home in any coffeehouse. Lightly drizzled with a delicate vanilla glaze, a quick dip in your coffee or tea will leave the beverage with an extra hint of sweetness to linger long after the cookie is gone.

APRICOT BISCOTTI:

1 cup dried apricots, chopped
1 cup almond meal
1 cup finely ground cornmeal
1 cup cornstarch
½ cup granulated sugar
½ teaspoon baking soda
½ cup vanilla vegan yogurt
¼ cup maple syrup
2 tablespoons olive oil
1 teaspoon vanilla extract

VANILLA GLAZE:

2 tablespoons vegan butter
½ cup confectioners' sugar
½ teaspoon vanilla extract

Preheat your oven to 325ºF (160ºC) and lightly grease two 9x5-inch loaf pans.

In a small saucepan over medium heat, cover the chopped apricots with water and bring to a boil. Reduce the heat and simmer for about 15 minutes, until most of the water has been absorbed. Drain any excess liquid and set the apricots aside to cool.

In a medium bowl, combine the almond meal, cornmeal, and cornstarch, stirring until combined. Mix in the granulated sugar and baking soda.

In a separate large bowl, stir together the yogurt, maple syrup, olive oil, and vanilla until smooth. Sift the dry ingredients into this bowl slowly, stirring until everything is completely combined with no lumps. You don't need to worry about overmixing, because there is no gluten involved! Finally, fold in the apricots that you had previously set aside.

Divide the dough evenly between the two loaf pans and pat it into the bottom, pressing the dough as smoothly as possible. Bake for 30 to 35 minutes, until lightly browned on the outside and cooked through the center. Let the biscotti loaves sit inside the pans for 10 minutes before turning them out onto a wire rack, where they should sit for an additional 15 minutes.

Raise the oven temperature to 350ºF (175ºC) and line a baking sheet with a silicone baking mat or parchment paper.

Slice the biscotti loaves into individual cookies, about ½-inch thick each. Lay the cookies with one of the cut sides down on the prepared baking sheet and bake for 15 minutes. Flip the biscotti over and bake for another 15 minutes. Cool the biscotti completely on a wire rack.

To finish them off, simply melt the butter and mix in the confectioners' sugar and vanilla until smooth. Drizzle this glaze over the biscotti. Alternately, you could dip the biscotti halfway into the icing for a sweeter finish.

Lend me your ears: Vegetable-based cookies may sound like a stretch, but fresh summer corn biscotti are more like hearty crackers, and truly something to savor. Lose the apricots altogether in favor of 1 cup corn kernels. Omit the sugar and vanilla but add 1 to 2 tablespoons finely minced fresh basil instead. A pinch of ground black pepper wouldn't hurt, while you're at it. Skip the glaze and pair with a creamy dip, like hummus or guacamole.

Black & White Cookies

Makes 12 to 14 large cookies

As a young child, my parents often took my sister and me into New York City to see the sights and experience a slice of the life that they once lived. Pounding down those concrete streets, peering up at buildings that never seemed to reach a peak, just being there was always a fantastic treat. However, at the end of the day, my favorite part came at a last-minute bakery run just before boarding the train back home. Among all the tempting pastries, lavished with twirls of billowing whipped cream and glittering with rainbow sprinkles, I could never deviate from the standard order of a jumbo black and white cookie. Every time it was the same thing, yet the repetition never wore on my taste buds. Now that the egg-based originals from New York are no longer an option, there is still no reason to go wanting. This updated classic tastes as authentic as anything you could find in or outside the city.

COOKIES:

2 cups all-purpose flour
1 teaspoon baking powder
½ teaspoon baking soda
¼ teaspoon salt
½ cup vegan butter
1 cup granulated sugar
1 tablespoon whole flaxseeds
2 tablespoons water
2 teaspoons vanilla extract
½ cup vegan sour cream or plain
   Greek-style vegan yogurt

VANILLA ICING:

2 cups confectioners' sugar
1–3 tablespoons aquafaba
¼ teaspoon vanilla extract

CHOCOLATE ICING:

3 ounces (about ½ cup) dark
   chocolate, roughly chopped
¼ cup unsweetened nondairy milk
1 tablespoon maple syrup
1 cup confectioners' sugar

Preheat your oven to 350°F (175°C) and line two baking sheets with silicone baking mats or parchment paper.

Sift together the flour, baking powder, baking soda, and salt in a medium bowl and set aside.

In your stand mixer, cream the butter and sugar until fluffy and fully combined. Grind the flaxseeds into a powder with a spice grinder, and mix with the water. Let stand for a few minutes to gelatinize. Add the flax mixture to your mixer. Incorporate the vanilla and sour cream, scraping down the sides of the bowl as necessary to achieve a completely smooth mixture. Slowly add in the flour mixture, stirring just enough to combine without any lumps remaining.

On the prepared baking sheets, drop about ¼ cup of dough for each cookie, leaving plenty of room for them to spread, roughly three inches between each. Use a cookie scoop or ice cream scooper for greater consistency. Lightly moisten your hands to prevent sticking and gently pat the dough mounds into approximately 2½-inch disks. Bake for 14 to 17 minutes, until they just begin to turn slightly golden in color. Let the cookies rest on the baking sheets for 2 more minutes before transferring them to a wire rack to cool completely.

For the vanilla icing, whisk together 1 cup of the confectioners' sugar in a small bowl with the first tablespoon of aquafaba and

vanilla, ensuring that you have a completely smooth mixture. Add in the remaining 1 cup of sugar and combine. Even though it may seem too dry at first, continue stirring and it will soon reveal itself as a nice, thick icing. Slowly drizzle in additional aquafaba if needed, but do so sparingly, as a little bit goes a long way. Set aside.

For the chocolate icing, place the chocolate, nondairy milk, and maple syrup in a microwave-safe bowl and heat for 30 to 60 seconds, just until the chocolate begins to melt. Stir vigorously to combine all the ingredients, until the chocolate is completely smooth. Set aside to cool and thicken slightly. Set aside.

Start by making the white side. Use a spatula to spread the vanilla icing on half of each cookie. Let the icing set for at least 10 minutes.

Returning to your chocolate icing, add in the 1 cup of confectioners' sugar and stir until completely smooth. Spread on the other half of each cookie. Let the cookies sit until the glaze has fully set up.

If you have a taste for darkness, try making *Half Moon Cookies*. This lesser-known variation is rumored to have begun in Utica, New York, where bakeries spike the soft cookie dough with a devilish extra dose of chocolate. Simply add ¼ cup Dutch-process cocoa powder to the batter to follow suit.

Black-Bottom Blondies

Makes 9 to 12 bars

Chocolate or vanilla? Brownies or blondies? There's no need to agonize over such tough choices when you can have them all in one bar! Not only is this a harmonious meeting of two worlds for the indecisive eater, but a gratifying compromise for the prolific baker as well, accomplishing two types of sweets at once without dirtying an extra pan! It's a win-win situation that's always a crowd-pleaser.

½ cup vegan butter

½ cup coconut sugar or dark brown sugar, firmly packed

½ cup granulated sugar

½ cup plain vegan yogurt

1 tablespoon vanilla extract

1¾ cups all-purpose flour

¼ teaspoon salt

¼ teaspoon baking soda

⅓ cup Dutch-process cocoa powder

¼ cup semisweet chocolate chips

¼ cup chopped, toasted pecans or walnuts

Preheat your oven to 350°F (175°C) and grease an 8x8-inch square baking pan.

Melt the butter over the stove top or in the microwave and stir in both sugars until dissolved. Let stand to cool for a minute or two before adding in the yogurt and vanilla extract. Mix well.

In a separate bowl, whisk together the flour, salt, and baking soda. Add the dry mixture to the wet and mix well.

Once the batter is homogenous, remove 1 cup and place it in a separate bowl. Stir the cocoa powder and chocolate chips into this portion, and smooth it into the bottom of your prepared dish. It will be very thick and sticky, so you may need to use lightly moistened hands or grease a flat spatula to press it properly into position.

Mix the toasted nuts into the remaining vanilla batter and pour the mixture over the chocolate base. Spread gently to completely and evenly cover the cocoa portion.

Bake for 28 to 35 minutes, until the sides pull away from the pan and the top turns golden brown. Let cool completely before cutting.

Butterscotch Blondies

Makes 9 to 12 bars

This particular childhood favorite turned out to be one of my greatest challenges in baking mastery. It should have been a breeze to deconstruct and re-create such an uncomplicated bite of nostalgia, inspired by memories of chewy little squares with lightly caramelized, crispy edges. And yet, my first attempt ended with a full pan of raw batter exploding mid-bake, smearing the walls of the oven with brown sugar napalm. I wish I were exaggerating, but many horrified witnesses can confirm the culinary tragedy that occurred on that day. Thankfully, the following 5 or 6 attempts only resulted in a trash can full of unsatisfactory baked goods rather than more spontaneous combustion. Now, I am happy to share a tried-and-true method, and it doesn't require you to blow anything up, either.

¼ cup vegan butter
1½ cups coconut sugar or dark
    brown sugar, firmly packed
2 teaspoons vanilla extract
½ cup plain vegan yogurt
⅓ cup full-fat coconut milk
2 cups all-purpose flour
2 teaspoons baking powder
½ teaspoon salt

Preheat your oven to 350°F (175°C) and lightly grease an 8x8-inch square baking pan.

Melt the butter and pour it over the sugar in a medium bowl, stirring to dissolve. Add the vanilla, yogurt, and coconut milk and mix until homogenous. Slowly incorporate the flour along with the baking powder and salt, stirring just enough to arrive at a smooth mixture. Pour the batter into your prepared pan. Bake for 25 to 30 minutes, until the sides just begin to pull away from the pan and the top is fairly firm. The blondies may still be slightly gooey on the inside, but they will continue to cook once removed from the oven. Besides, they are "fudgy" bars, so you don't want them to dry out! Wait for the blondies to cool completely before cutting.

If you have leftover filling, don't let it go to waste! Use it as spread for toast, a dip to pair with sliced apples, or stir it into oatmeal for a special breakfast treat.

Cheesecake Thumbprint Cookies

Makes approximately 16 to 20 cookies

Arguably even better than individual cheesecakes, each two-bite indulgence is a suitable ending to any meal, or the start of any snack, for that matter. You don't even need to pull up a chair or grab a fork to dig in! Perfect on the go or with a tall cup of coffee, these no-fuss sweets are much easier to make, bring to events, and devour after a substantial meal than an imposing, dense slice. If you'd like to really get the party started with another layer of flavor, try topping them with your favorite jam or preserves.

CHEESECAKE FILLING:

4 ounces (½ cup) vegan cream cheese

¼ cup granulated sugar

⅛ teaspoon salt

1 tablespoon plain nondairy milk

¼ teaspoon vanilla extract

1 teaspoon arrowroot powder

COOKIE:

½ cup vegan butter

¼ cup granulated sugar

1 tablespoon ground flaxseeds

2 tablespoons water

1 cup finely ground graham crackers (about 6 full rectangles)

1 cup all-purpose flour

Preheat your oven to 350°F (175°C) and line two baking sheets with silicone baking mats or parchment paper.

To prepare the filling, begin by stirring the cream cheese with a spatula in a medium bowl to soften it a bit. Add in the sugar and salt, and cream thoroughly. Incorporate the nondairy milk and vanilla, mixing until you have a completely homogenous mixture. Stirring rapidly, sprinkle in the arrowroot, mixing until smooth and creamy once more. Set aside.

For the cookie, use your stand mixer to cream the butter and sugar together. Mix together the ground flax and water before adding them into the bowl. Stir thoroughly to combine. Add in the ground graham crackers first, making sure they are fully incorporated before adding the flour. Be careful to mix it for just long enough to bring the dough together, lest you want some tough cookies.

Scoop out balls of dough that are about an inch or so in diameter, rolling them into fairly smooth spheres with your hands. Place on your prepared baking sheets and either use your fingers or the handle of a wooden spoon to make an indentation in the center of each. Bake the cookies for 10 minutes before checking on their progress. If your indentations are on the shallow side, you should take this opportunity to press the centers back in and reshape any other abnormalities. Bake for another 5 to 7 minutes, until they just begin to brown.

Remove the cookies from the oven with your filling at the ready. Spoon 2 to 3 teaspoons of cheesecake filling into the centers, and return them once more to the oven to bake for an additional 8 minutes or so. The filling will begin to puff up a bit and will solidify when they are done. Let the cookies sit for 2 minutes on the sheet before moving them to a wire rack to finish cooling.

Coffee Break Shortbread

Makes 12 to 16 cookies

Long school days followed by interminable hours of homework have taught me at least one important lesson: never plan an all-nighter without arming yourself with a bottomless mug of strong coffee. Better yet, grab a stack of cookies with that same addictive flavor and the energizing boost of caffeine baked inside! Whip up a double (or triple) batch of these invigorating morsels for your longest study sessions to stay focused, or at least sweetly satisfied.

½ cup confectioners' sugar
½ cup vegan butter
1 tablespoon instant coffee granules or powder
1 teaspoon vanilla extract
1 cup all-purpose flour
¼ teaspoon salt

Cream together the sugar and butter in your stand mixer, followed by the instant coffee and vanilla. Slowly mix in the flour and salt until it starts to become incorporated. You may need to run your mixer for a minute, rest the dough, then mix again to create smooth results. The dough will start off looking very crumbly and dry, but resist the urge to add liquid; it will come together if you give it time! Once you have a solid, cohesive ball of dough, refrigerate it for at least an hour.

Pull the dough from the refrigerator, preheat your oven to 325°F (160°C), and line two baking sheets with silicone baking mats or parchment paper.

Roll out the dough using a rolling pin lightly coated in flour to prevent sticking; ⅛ inch in thickness is ideal. Cut the dough into your desired shapes using cookie cutters and place the cookies onto your prepared baking sheets. Baking time can vary greatly, from 14 minutes and up depending on the size of your shapes, so keep a close eye on their progress. Don't wait for them to brown very much, but they should be somewhat firm to the touch when done. Remove the cookies from the baking sheet to cool.

> If you're more of a "tea"-totaler, try using roughly crushed green or black tea leaves instead of instant coffee.

Crumb-Topped Brownies

Makes 9 to 12 brownies

Whenever I baked my chocolate streusel cupcakes, everyone would rave about the sweet, cocoa crumb topping even more than the tender cake underneath. Hungry for a change of pace when tasked to produce yet another pan of standard brownies, it was an epiphany when I realized the solution was right in front of me. In short time, the best part of those two sweets were happily married in harmonious chocolate bliss. Though it's always tempting to pick the crunchy sugared crust off the top of any unknown dessert, what lies beneath is every bit as ambrosial.

CRUMB TOPPING:

¼ cup granulated sugar

¼ cup Dutch-process cocoa powder

¼ cup all-purpose flour

2 tablespoons olive oil

BROWNIES:

¼ cup vegan butter

½ cup plain vegan yogurt

½ cup coconut sugar or dark brown sugar, firmly packed

¼ cup granulated sugar

½ teaspoon instant coffee granules or powder (optional)

1 teaspoon vanilla extract

¾ cup all-purpose flour

½ cup Dutch-process cocoa powder

¼ teaspoon salt

¼ teaspoon baking soda

3 ounces (½ cup) semisweet chocolate chips

Preheat your oven to 350ºF (175ºC) and grease an 8x8-inch square baking pan.

To make the topping, combine the granulated sugar, cocoa, and flour in a small bowl. Add in the oil and stir with a fork, breaking up the topping into small- and medium-sized crumbs. Set aside.

For the batter, melt the butter and allow a few minutes for it to cool down a bit before using. In a stand mixer, combine the yogurt and both sugars, followed by the melted butter. Stir thoroughly before mixing in the coffee powder (if using) and vanilla as well. Add in the flour, cocoa, salt, and baking soda. Pause occasionally to allow the mixer to catch up, but rest assured that it will all come together in due time. Fold in the chips by hand and smooth the batter into your prepared pan.

Sprinkle your crumb topping liberally on top and bake for 22 to 26 minutes, until the sides pull away from the pan slightly. Allow the brownies to cool completely before cutting.

Lace Florentines

Makes approximately 48 separate crisps or 24 cookie sandwiches

Simple, sweet, and shatteringly crisp, each elegant caramelized cookie could make a gorgeous accompaniment to fresh berry parfaits or scoops of ice cream. Smear a thick layer of chocolate between two of those dainty disks, and now you've suddenly got a solo showstopper on your hands. Still hot out of the oven, the pliable rounds can also wrap up in tightly curled cigars, or molded over metal cupcake tins to make edible bowls. It's hard to beat the standard sandwich though, which has the ideal ratio of chocolate to cookie, in my opinion.

¼ cup vegan butter
¼ cup dark brown sugar, firmly packed
¼ cup dark agave nectar
¼ cup all-purpose flour
2 tablespoons almond meal
2 tablespoons instant oatmeal
⅛ teaspoon salt
3 ounces (½ cup) semisweet chocolate chips (optional)

Preheat your oven to 375°F (190°C) and line two baking sheets with silicone baking mats or parchment paper.

Heat the butter, sugar, and agave nectar together in a small saucepan over medium-low heat. Remove from the heat once the butter has completely melted, and vigorously whisk in the flour, almond meal, oatmeal, and salt to avoid clumps.

Drop about ½ teaspoon of batter per cookie onto your prepared baking sheets. Take care to place them several inches apart, as they spread like crazy. Bake the crisps for 5 to 6 minutes, until they are caramelized and bubbly, keeping a close eye on them the entire time they're in the oven. They will still be soft and malleable at first; wait a few minutes for the crisps to cool and solidify before handling. They are very fragile after they harden, so be gentle!

If desired, melt the chocolate in the microwave in 30-second intervals, stirring thoroughly until completely melted and smooth. Smear a thin layer of the melted chocolate on the underside of one cookie, sandwiching it between a second. Alternatively, drizzle the chocolate all over the individual crisps, Jackson Pollak-style.

Store cookies in an airtight container at room temperature. Heat and moisture will change their texture, so the crisps may remain slightly soft if you are baking in a very humid climate.

Maple Pistachio Crèmes

Makes 20 to 24 sandwich cookies

What's a food photographer's favorite subject? Pistachios, because they're always smiling!

Bad jokes aside, Persians have called pistachios "the smiling nuts" for centuries because the split shell resembles a smile. The Chinese simply refer to it as "the happy nut," which is also appropriate, because their delicate flavor and crisp crunch always brings me joy.

Pistachio fan that I am, I find it frustrating that this beautiful nut is rarely utilized by most home cooks. Flavorful and agreeable with a cornucopia of other flavors, be it sweet or savory, the hardest part about working with these shelled treasures is choosing what else to pair them with. In this case, I really wanted the pistachio to finally get its fair share of the spotlight, accentuating it with the woodsy, earthy sweetness of maple syrup. Crunchy, creamy, and with a bold green hue that artifical colors can only dream of imitating, these cookies could make a pistachio lover out of anyone.

COOKIES:
½ cup vegan butter or
    coconut oil
⅔ cup maple syrup
2¾ cups all-purpose flour
1 teaspoon baking powder
1 teaspoon vanilla extract
¼ teaspoon lemon extract
    or lemon zest
¼ teaspoon salt

PISTACHIO CRÈME:
1 cup shelled, toasted
    pistachios or ⅔ cup
    pistachio butter
¼ cup full-fat coconut milk
3 tablespoons maple syrup
½ teaspoon vanilla

Preheat your oven to 350ºF (175ºC) and line two baking sheets with silicone baking mats or parchment paper.

In a large microwave-safe bowl, melt the butter or coconut oil and then stir in the maple syrup. Add in 2 cups of the flour, along with the baking powder, vanilla, lemon extract or zest, and salt. Stir the batter until all the ingredients are fully combined. Add in the remainder of the flour and combine. The batter should be rather thick; resist the temptation to add more liquid.

Scoop out walnut-sized balls and roll them in your hands to make them nicely rounded. Place the balls onto your prepared baking sheets about 1 inch apart. Bake for 10 to 12 minutes, but don't wait for them to brown. Once the cookies firm up a bit, and no longer appear moist on top, they are done! Let the cookies cool on the sheets.

To make the pistachio crème, toss the pistachios into your food processor and grind them on full power for up to 10 minutes, so that they become relatively smooth and paste-like. The mixture will start out as a coarse meal, break down to a finer powder, and eventually turn into a smooth paste. The process will take some time, and you may need to pause to scrape down the sides of the container with a spatula—just stick with it! Once smooth, keep the motor running and slowly drizzle in the coconut milk, followed by the maple syrup and vanilla. Process until fully incorporated. If using ready-made pistachio butter, simply mix together all the ingredients until completely smooth.

After the cookies have cooled, spoon a dollop of the crème (about 1 to 2 teaspoons) onto the flat side of one cookie, and top with a second. Repeat with the remaining cookies.

Nut Case Cookies

Makes 36 cookies

I often buy huge bags of nuts at a time, which is great for larger recipes, but when I get down to the bottom, there's never enough of one to satisfy any recipe alone. Utilizing all those scrappy remnants, the sum is far greater than its parts. What follows is my favorite combination made with the components I most frequently keep, but in the spirit of salvaging otherwise idle leftovers, feel free create your own adventure based on the concept. Substitute whatever nuts you have on hand, whole or chopped, raw or roasted. You could even go a bit "nuts" and throw in a splash of almond extract!

1 cup vegan butter
½ cup granulated sugar
½ cup coconut sugar or dark brown sugar, firmly packed
1 cup whole wheat pastry flour
1½ cups all-purpose flour
1 teaspoon baking soda
½ teaspoon salt
1 teaspoon vanilla extract
¼ cup aquafaba
½ cup toasted almonds, roughly chopped
½ cup toasted cashews, roughly chopped
½ cup toasted pistachios, roughly chopped

Preheat your oven to 350°F (175°C) and line two baking sheets with silicone baking mats or parchment paper.

In your stand mixer, cream together the butter and both sugars. In a separate bowl, combine the two flours, baking soda, and salt. Slowly incorporate the dry ingredients into the mixer until everything is combined. Add the vanilla and aquafaba next, mixing so that the dough is completely homogenous through and through. Fold in the nuts by hand to distribute evenly.

Drop rounded tablespoons of dough onto your prepared baking sheets, allowing plenty of room for them to spread. Bake for 10 to 14 minutes, until the cookies are no longer shiny on top. Remove them from the baking sheet immediately and allow them to cool.

Orange Hazelnut Biscotti

Makes 12 to 15 biscotti

Orange is the new biscotti, don't you know? More compelling than a passing fashion trend or viral pop culture hit, this citrus is king, goes with everything, and won't be forgotten with next season's programming. Hazelnut and chocolate have a proven affinity across decades of culinary flights of fancy and pastry binge watching, which garners the trio top ratings on the cookie plate. Bright flecks of fresh orange zest bring these crunchy biscotti to life, in vivid flavor that unquestionably exceeds the abilities of high-definition TV.

½ cup vegan butter
¾ cup granulated sugar
1 tablespoon ground flaxseeds
2 tablespoons water
1 tablespoon orange zest
2 cups all-purpose flour
1½ teaspoons baking powder
¼ teaspoon salt
½ cup toasted hazelnuts, roughly chopped
¼ cup orange juice
6 ounces (about 1 cup) dark chocolate, roughly chopped

Preheat your oven to 350°F (175°C) and line a baking sheet with a silicone baking mat or parchment paper.

Cream the butter in your mixer, beating until light and fluffy. Add in the sugar and mix until fully incorporated. Separately, stir the flaxseeds together with the water to form a paste. Add to the mixer and thoroughly blend. Toss in the zest from your orange and mix again. Sift in the flour, baking powder, and salt, mixing lightly until relatively combined. Continuing with the mixer on a slow speed, drop in the hazelnuts, and slowly drizzle the orange juice into the mixture until it just comes together in a cohesive ball.

Shape the resulting dough into a long, skinny rectangle, about 1 inch tall and 2 inches wide; the length isn't so critical. Place it onto your prepared baking sheet and bake for 35 to 40 minutes.

The top of the biscotti loaf should be lightly browned, but don't panic if it seems a little bit soft and bread-like on the inside. Cool for at least 15 minutes before slicing, using a very sharp knife to cut horizontally into pieces that are about ½- to ¾-inch thick. Lay the slices down flat on one of the cut sides on the baking sheet and return the biscotti to the oven for another 10 minutes. Flip them over onto the opposite side and bake for another 10 minutes. Allow the biscotti to cool completely.

Place the chocolate in a relatively shallow, microwave-safe dish that can accommodate the full length of the cookies. In the microwave, heat your chocolate in 30-second intervals, stirring well after each period until completely smooth. Dip each biscotto into the chocolate and place it back on a silicone baking mat or parchment paper. Allow the chocolate to fully set before removing them again.

Party Mix Bars

Makes 20 to 24 bars

Friends coming over unexpectedly for a movie night, game of Scrabble, video games, or just to hang out? Don't drag out that tired old bag of snack mix; whip up a festive batch of bars liable to become the life of the party! This sweet and salty treat takes shape as grabbable, munchable squares, rather than a handful of loose munchies, leaving less mess to collect between sofa cushions the next day. A single batch can accommodate a ravenous crowd and is no more laborious than making banal crispy rice treats. What are you waiting for? When they find out what's in store, your guests will be at your door before you know it!

2 cups mini pretzel twists and/
or sticks
2 cups corn and/or wheat
cereal squares
3 cups crispy rice cereal
1½ cups roasted and salted
mixed nuts
1 tablespoon vegan butter
¾ cup granulated sugar
1 cup light agave nectar or
maple syrup
1 teaspoon vanilla extract

Combine the pretzels, both types of cereal, and nuts in a large bowl. Liberally coat a 9x13-inch baking pan with cooking spray. Set both aside.

Set a medium saucepan over low heat and begin by melting the butter alone. Once it has liquefied, add in the sugar and syrup, stirring as necessary until the sugar crystals dissolve. Turn up the heat and bring the mixture to a steady boil. Cook for an additional 3 to 5 minutes, until it appears to have thickened slightly. Remove from the heat and quickly stir in the vanilla. Pour the contents of your saucepan over the dry mix and fold it in carefully but briskly, being careful not to crush the cereal.

Pour everything into your prepared pan and gently press it out into an even layer. Let cool completely before cutting into bars.

> If nuts aren't invited to this party, use crispy dry roasted chickpeas or soybeans instead.

Peanut Butter Bombs

Makes 12 to 14 cookies

They may look like plain old chocolate cookies from the outside, but one bite will reveal an explosion of rich, crunchy peanut butter! Seriously satisfying, like a peanut butter cup in cookie form, these are perhaps the only bomb that I can condone making.

PEANUT BUTTER FILLING:

¼ cup crunchy peanut butter

⅓ cup confectioners' sugar

1 teaspoon unsweetened nondairy milk

CHOCOLATE-PEANUT BUTTER COOKIE:

¼ cup vegan butter

¼ cup creamy peanut butter

⅓ cup dark brown sugar, firmly packed

⅓ cup granulated sugar

½ cup plain or vanilla vegan yogurt

1 tablespoon unsweetened non-dairy milk

1 teaspoon vanilla extract

1¼ cups all-purpose flour

½ cup Dutch-process cocoa powder

¼ teaspoon baking soda

¼ teaspoon salt

> Blow up your holiday cookie exchange with a cinnamon speculoos blast! Use either creamy or crunchy speculoos spread (also known as cookie butter) instead of peanut butter for a critical seasonal hit.

Preheat your oven to 350ºF (175ºC) and line two baking sheets with silicone baking mats or parchment paper.

In a small bowl, combine all the ingredients for the filling and stir well. It should have a crumbly consistency, but still hold together when pressed. Once everything is fully incorporated, set aside.

In your mixer, cream together the butter, peanut butter, and both sugars. Mix in the yogurt, nondairy milk, and vanilla, and continue beating until smooth. In a separate bowl, combine the flour, cocoa powder, baking soda, and salt. Slowly add these dry ingredients into the wet, being careful not to overmix.

The dough may be rather sticky at first. If you have trouble shaping it, let it rest in the refrigerator for about 30 minutes, or try moistening your hands slightly before handling.

For each cookie, roll about a tablespoon of dough into a ball and press it down flat onto your silicone baking mat or parchment paper. Line the cookies up 3 x 3 on your two baking sheets, with plenty of room in between. Drop a rounded teaspoon or so of your peanut butter filling into the center of each, and top with another flattened round of dough. Be sure to cover the whole dollop of filling, pressing the edges together, making sure that the two pieces form a complete seal all around the cookie. Bake for 8 to 12 minutes, until the cookies no longer appear shiny on top. Remove the cookies from the oven and allow them to cool on the baking sheet.

Peanut-Plus Cookies

Makes 24 cookies

All signs would seem to say these are your typical tasty peanut butter cookies: endearingly nutty, soft, and chewy, unmistakably speckled with crunchy roasted nuts throughout. Every aspect of this classification is accurate, although there is something slightly different about these cookies that most eaters wouldn't venture to guess. Lentils and potatoes are the secret ingredients added to this mix, negating the need for wheat altogether. Challenge the cookie status quo with a more diverse arsenal of ingredients, and you won't be disappointed.

½ cup red lentils, dry
½ cup plain nondairy milk
¼ cup potato flour
1 cup crunchy peanut butter
¾ cup granulated sugar
¼ cup cornstarch
2 teaspoons cream of tartar
1 teaspoon baking soda
1 teaspoon vanilla extract
¼ teaspoon salt

Preheat your oven to 350ºF (175ºC) and line two baking sheets with silicone baking mats or parchment paper.

Begin by grinding up your dry lentils in a food processor for a good 5 to 10 minutes, until they become a fine powder. This step is crucial, as any larger fragments will change the texture of the finished cookies substantially. If you do not have a food processor handy, then the lentils can be ground in a spice grinder in about two batches.

While your lentils are churning away, combine the nondairy milk and potato flour in a microwave-safe bowl and heat for one minute. Let the potato mixture cool for a minute or two, before tossing it into a stand mixer along with your freshly processed lentil flour. Mix in the peanut butter and sugar. Sprinkle in the cornstarch while keeping your mixer on low, increasing the speed once everything is combined and no longer threatens to send starch flying out. Make sure the dough is thoroughly mixed before introducing the remaining ingredients. Stir until completely smooth.

Spoon rounded tablespoons of dough onto the prepared baking sheets. Leave a good amount of room between the cookies to allow for spreading, but they shouldn't spread too far; about an inch should do the trick. Bake for 10 to 12 minutes, until they are no longer shiny on top, but have not yet begun to brown around the edges. To ensure a soft, chewy cookie, remove the cookies from the oven just before they begin to take on color. Allow them to sit on the hot baking sheet for another 5 minutes before pulling the silicone baking mat off onto a cooler surface.

Pfeffernusse

Makes 20 to 24 cookies

German "pepper nuts" take soft gingerbread bites and spike them with a bold punch of warm spices, accented by the distinctive licorice-like flavor of anise. Lovers of chai tea will also fall in love with these tender sugar-coated morsels thanks to the fragrant hint of cardamom carried throughout. Condensing such a diverse world of flavors into such small packages, these classic holiday treats are long overdue for a revival across the globe. You may find it difficult to sacrifice any of these delights to leave out for Santa, let alone share with your friends!

½ cup vegan butter
½ cup granulated sugar
2 tablespoons molasses
2 tablespoons aquafaba
¾ teaspoon pure anise extract or
    ½ teaspoon ground anise seeds
1¼ cups all-purpose flour
½ cup almond meal
1 teaspoon baking powder
¼ teaspoon baking soda
¼ teaspoon salt
¾ teaspoon ground cinnamon
¼ teaspoon ground cloves
¼ teaspoon ground cardamom
¼ teaspoon ground black pepper
About 1 cup confectioners' sugar,
    to coat

In your stand mixer, cream the butter and sugar together until light and fluffy. Scrape down the side of the bowl to prevent any lumps from being left behind. Beat in the molasses and aquafaba, followed shortly by the anise.

Combine the flour, almond meal, baking powder, baking soda, salt, and dry spices in a large bowl. Gradually add this flour mixture to the mixer. Stir slowly until a cohesive dough begins to form, so that the dry ingredients don't fly out and decorate your kitchen walls with spicy holiday cheer. Manually press the dough into a ball and wrap it tightly in plastic before placing it into the refrigerator for at least 30 minutes.

When it is time to remove the dough from the refrigerator, preheat your oven to 350°F (175°C) and line two baking sheets with silicone baking mats or parchment paper.

Roll the dough into 1-inch balls, handling them as little as possible. Place them about two inches apart on your prepared baking sheets. Bake for 10 to 12 minutes, until the cookies are lightly but evenly browned.

Once they come out of the oven, roll the cookies in a dish full of confectioners' sugar and cool them on a wire rack. The cookies may absorb the sugar over time, so you might wish to coat them a second time to achieve a brighter snowball appearance before serving.

Strawberry Spirals

Makes 36 to 48 cookies

Everyone's familiar with the standard cast of characters inevitably taking up residence on your average holiday cookie platter, rarely deviating from the tried-and-true crowd pleasers. Soft sugar cookies, gingersnaps, and peanut butter buckeyes are always in attendance, never tardy. Shortbread, almond spritz, and lemon drops dress up in their winter finest, putting on a good show as always. Sure, the mesmerizing chocolate pinwheels that grace many a plate are perfectly agreeable little corkscrews, though their flavor never lives up to such visual promise. Rather than sacrificing taste for design, why not roll up some flavorful fruit, like brilliant red strawberries? To keep with the Christmas theme, feel free to substitute dried cranberries instead for a tart, tangy, and festive variation.

FRUIT FILLING:

2 cups dried strawberries
⅓ cup water
1 teaspoon cornstarch

COOKIE DOUGH:

1 cup vegan butter
½ cup granulated sugar
1 teaspoon vanilla extract
2¼ cups all-purpose flour
½ cup whole wheat pastry flour
2 tablespoons cornstarch
¼ teaspoon baking powder
¼ teaspoon baking soda
¼ teaspoon salt
3–5 tablespoons lemon juice

½ cup decorative pearl sugar,
    sanding sugar, or turbinado
    sugar (optional)

In your food processor or blender, blend together the dried strawberries and water until mostly smooth. Slowly sprinkle in the cornstarch with the motor running, in order to prevent lumps from forming. Set aside.

In your stand mixer, cream together the butter and sugar until light and fluffy. Mix in the vanilla and beat until fully combined. In a separate bowl, whisk together both flours, cornstarch, baking powder, baking soda, and salt. Slowly add this flour mixture to your batter and mix just until combined. Drizzle in the lemon juice until the dough achieves a workable consistency. It should be very stiff and firm, but moist enough to hold together when pressed.

Divide the dough into two even halves and form each into a rectangle as best you can. Wrap the rectangles in plastic wrap, and let them rest in the refrigerator for at least 2 hours.

Once thoroughly chilled, remove one piece of dough from the refrigerator and roll it out between two sheets of parchment paper to about ¼-inch thick. Try to keep it as rectangular as possible. Peel away one piece of the parchment and gently spread the strawberry mixture atop your dough, leaving a border of about ½ inch without fruit around edges. Starting with a long side of the dough, roll it into a log, using the parchment as leverage, and being careful not to mash the filling. Repeat this process with the second rectangle. Re-wrap these logs in plastic wrap and chill in the freezer for another few hours, until solid

(continued on next page)

but pliable. I find that the dough will hold its shape better if you stick it inside a cardboard paper towel roll that has been split down the middle, but it should be okay even if you don't go to this trouble.

Once the dough is properly chilled, preheat your oven to 350°F (175°C) and line two baking sheets with silicone baking mats or fresh parchment paper.

Using a serrated knife carefully cut the logs crosswise into ⅓- to ½-inch-thick slices. Use a sawing motion with the knife, trying not to apply significant pressure. Place the slices on the prepared baking sheets with a good amount of room around them, about an inch or so. Bake for 15 to 17 minutes, until the cookies just begin to lightly brown around the edges. Remove from the oven, and let the cookies sit for one additional minute before transferring them to a wire rack for further cooling.

> Really get into the holiday spirit by incorporating 2 teaspoons of matcha into the cookie dough. The contrasting green color will be bright and merry against the red fruit filling, to say nothing of the joyous green tea astringency.

Turtle Shortbread Wedges

Makes 16 cookies

Rich, velvety chocolate, dark caramelized sugar, and crunchy toasted pecans were simply made for each other. The "turtle" moniker for this unbeatable trio came from palm-sized candies originally shaped somewhat like their namesake animal. Though cute in a crude sort of way, I can't understand why you'd want to eat a turtle in the first place, even if it was a sweet confection. Titles aside, this combination of ingredients is a real knockout, reptilian in nature or not. Proceed with caution: Such a decadent assemblage has been known to elicit moans of pleasure just upon first sight, and whole batches of this layered cookie sensation have been known to mysteriously disappear overnight.

CHOCOLATE SHORTBREAD:

½ cup vegan butter

¼ cup dark brown sugar, firmly packed

1 teaspoon vanilla extract

¼ teaspoon salt

1 cup all-purpose flour

¼ cup Dutch-process cocoa powder

CARAMEL TOPPING:

2 cups granulated sugar

¼ teaspoon cream of tartar

¼ teaspoon salt

⅓ cup water

¼ cup full-fat coconut milk

1¼ cups lightly toasted pecan halves

Preheat your oven to 350ºF (175ºC) and generously grease an 8-inch round springform pan.

For the shortbread, cream the butter and sugar together in your stand mixer until soft and fluffy. Add in the vanilla and salt. Turn the mixer off to add in both the flour and cocoa powder, starting it up at a slow speed to prevent a cloud of dry ingredients from flying right out. It may take a little bit of mixing for everything to come together, but be patient and resist the urge to add liquid.

Press the dough into the bottom of your prepared pan. It will be very thick and stiff, so you may want to grease your hands or use a piece of wax paper to smooth it in. Cover the bottom of the pan evenly and completely. Bake for 20 minutes, until the dough appears firmer on top, and the sides look a bit crispy. If you are not sure if it is done by that time, trust your intuition and take it out after an additional minute at most. It is hard to distinguish "done" from "burnt" when it starts out as such a dark color in the first place.

While the shortbread is baking, begin to prepare the caramel topping. Take out a medium saucepan and place your sugar, cream of tartar, salt, and water inside. Set it over medium heat and stir the mixture just to combine, after which time you must not agitate it for about 5 to 7 minutes. Once it turns a shade of light amber, it will continue to color very quickly, so stay on your toes! (At this point, your shortbread should be out of the

(continued on page 97)

oven and nearby, ready to go) Stir occasionally until it reaches the hard-crack stage at 300ºF (150ºC). If you don't have a candy thermometer handy, drop a small amount of the syrup into a cup of cold water to test. It should form thin, brittle threads that break if you try to bend them. Stand back from the stove slightly while still stirring, and pour in the coconut milk with care, as it could splash back violently. Stir in the pecans just to combine. Turn off the heat, and pour the whole mixture over the chocolate shortbread.

Return the pan to your oven for 10 more minutes, until the caramel has darkened slightly. Let it cool for at least 20 minutes before running a knife around the edge to loosen. Release the springform sides to transfer the full cookie disk out onto a cutting board, and cut into wedges while it is still slightly warm. Let cool completely before serving or storing.

Whoopie Pies

Makes 8 to 10 large sandwich cookies or 15 to 18 minis

Wrapped up in plastic like hazardous material and sporting ingredient lists that read more like failed science experiments than food, my earliest exposure to whoopie pies at a gas station pit stop was not exactly compelling. I couldn't wrap my mind around the appeal of squishy, week-old cake wrapped around achingly sweet frosting, piled up on the counter like a basket of brown tennis balls. It took many more years to find the subject worthy of reexamination, not to mention a total gut-renovation. Baked from scratch and eaten fresh, this soft chocolate cookie sandwich gets a whole new lease on life.

CHOCOLATE COOKIES:
1 cup unsweetened nondairy milk
1 teaspoon apple cider vinegar
1 cup whole wheat pastry flour
1 cup all-purpose flour
½ cup Dutch-process cocoa
    powder
1 teaspoon baking powder
1 teaspoon baking soda
½ teaspoon salt
½ cup vegan butter
¼ cup granulated sugar
½ cup dark brown sugar, firmly
    packed
2 tablespoons vegan sour cream or
    plain vegan yogurt
1 teaspoon vanilla extract

CRÈME FILLING:
2 cups confectioners' sugar
⅓ cup vegan butter
1–3 tablespoons unsweetened
    nondairy milk
1 teaspoon vanilla extract

Preheat your oven to 350°F (175°C) and line two baking sheets with silicone baking mats or parchment paper.

In a small bowl, whisk together the nondairy milk and vinegar and let stand about 5 minutes. Separately, in a medium bowl, whisk together the flours, cocoa powder, baking powder, baking soda, and salt. Set aside.

In your stand mixer, cream together the vegan butter and both sugars, beating to ensure that the contents of the bowl are creamy and fully combined. Add the sour cream or yogurt and mix again to incorporate, even if the resulting mixture isn't exactly smooth.

Returning to the bowl of milk, whisk in the vanilla. Beginning with these wet ingredients, alternately add them with the dry ingredients into your mixer. Scrape down the sides of the bowl with a spatula as necessary to incorporate everything, stirring the batter just enough to fully combine.

Use an ice cream scoop or measuring cup to drop 3 to 4 tablespoons for large cookies, or about 1 tablespoon each to make minis. Drop the dough onto your prepared baking sheets, leaving a good amount of space between each cookie to allow them to spread a bit; about 2 inches for the large, 1 inch for minis. Bake for 10 to 14 minutes if large (8 to 12 if mini), until they're no longer shiny on top. Remove the cookies from the oven and let them cool completely on the baking sheets, where they should firm up a bit more.

(continued on next page)

To make the filling, begin with the mixer on low and beat together the confectioners' sugar and butter. Add the first tablespoon of nondairy milk along with the vanilla. Once the sugar is safely incorporated, turn the mixer up to high and whip for a good 2 or 3 minutes; this will incorporate more air, making for a lighter, fluffier filling. Slowly drizzle in additional milk only if needed to create a spreadable but sturdy consistency.

Drop a healthy dollop of the crème mixture onto the flat side of one cooled cookie and place the flat side of a second cookie on top. Press down gently to bring the filling right out to the edge. Repeat this process with your remaining cookies and crème filling.

Whoopie pies enjoyed a fleeting moment of mainstream fame right as the cupcake craze died down, leading to a flood of creative new twists on the usual chocolate and vanilla affair. *Red Velvet* indisputably skyrocketed to the top of that list in terms of popularity, and it's an equally delightful departure from this standard formula. To re-create that scarlet starlet, use natural cocoa and reduce it to just 2 tablespoons, while increasing the all-purpose flour to 1⅓ cups total. Swap the nondairy milk for beet juice to get that brilliant but completely natural hue. Add 3 tablespoons of cream cheese into the filling to really put the icing on the cake—or *in* the cake, as it were.

CAKES & CUPCAKES

*Apple juice concentrate is readily available in the freezer aisle of most grocery stores but can also be made at home with a bit of patience and an abundance of fresh juice. Simply place 100 percent unsweetened apple juice or cider in a large stock pot and simmer gently until reduced by about half. That means you will need to start with at least 4 cups of juice to have enough for one batch of cake.

Apple Spice Cake

Makes 10 to 12 servings

Dietary restrictions are no obstacle in my eyes, but instead are challenges that inspire me to push beyond the usual routine. In this case, it wasn't one of the predictable culprits like nuts or gluten throwing down the gauntlet. My Nana, one of the sweetest people I know, is ironically, lamentably diabetic. She managed to turn her life around and completely regain her health through diet and exercise, and refined sugars and flours are completely out of the question these days. When her birthday rolls around, though, it tortured me to arrive at the party empty handed.

Using only fruit and whole grains to concoct a treat sounds dubious at best, but this towering naked cake goes au naturel, without shame or reluctance. Even the kids who might otherwise lean toward candy-coated neon sprinkles dig in with voracious appetites. Of course, the birthday girl was over the moon with her customized slice, but that came as no surprise; she's already sweet enough as is.

APPLE SPICE CAKE:

2 cups whole wheat pastry flour
2 cups old-fashioned rolled oats
2 teaspoons ground cinnamon
½ teaspoon ground nutmeg
½ teaspoon ground cloves
1 teaspoon baking powder
1½ teaspoons baking soda
½ teaspoon salt
½ cup olive oil
2 cups 100% apple juice concentrate, thawed and undiluted*
½ cup unsweetened applesauce
1 tablespoon apple cider vinegar
2 teaspoons vanilla extract
3 medium-sized fuji or gala apples, divided
1 cup raisins
1 cup chopped walnuts

TOPPING:

1 cup Apple Butter (page 227)

Preheat your oven to 350°F (175°C) and grease two 8-inch round cake pans.

Combine the flour, oats, spices, baking powder, baking soda, and salt in a large bowl and set aside. In your stand mixer, blend the olive oil with the juice concentrate, followed by the applesauce, vinegar, and vanilla. Mix well. It might look a bit lumpy and unappealing, but have no fear! It will quickly improve from this point on, I promise.

With your mixer on low speed, to avoid sending flour flying onto the walls, slowly add in the dry ingredients. Be careful not to overmix. Peel, core, and dice two of the apples. Fold the apple bits, along with the raisins and nuts, into the mixture. Once the goodies are well distributed, spread the batter into your greased pans. This is a very thick batter, so you may have to press it into shape with a spatula to evenly fill each pan.

Core the last remaining apple and slice it very, very thinly for the topping. Use a mandoline if you have it for greater accuracy and consistency. Arrange the slices around the edge, slightly overlapping, on top of only one cake layer. Depending on the size of the apple, you may have some leftover; have yourself a little snack!

Bake for 30 to 40 minutes, until a toothpick inserted into the center of each layer comes out clean.

Let the layers cool to room temperature inside the pans. Turn the first layer out onto the plate you want to serve it on before slathering it with Apple Butter. Smooth the spread out almost to the edge but not quite, as the weight of the top layer will press it out further. Place the second layer on top and have a taste of sweetness without the sugar rush!

Bananas Foster Cake

Makes 10 to 12 servings

Banana cake is all too often a disappointment. Dry as a brick, austere as a bran muffin, many people think it's perfectly all right to use any old banana bread recipe, slap some frosting on top, and call it dessert. Bananas can do so much better, given the freedom to embrace their sweeter side! Taking a page from the showstopping grand finale that is bananas Foster, these tender layers are soaked in rum before assembly and topped with a subtly salted caramel frosting that pulls the whole dessert together. In the typical showy fashion of the original, the garnish could be made with the addition of some rum and set ablaze to let the alcohol cook off. Knowing my personal ineptitude with fire, though, I think it is safer to recommend a simple sauté. The end results are still extraordinary, even without the stove-top conflagration.

BANANA CAKE:

2½ cups all-purpose flour
2 teaspoons baking powder
2 teaspoons baking soda
½ teaspoon salt
⅔ cup unsweetened nondairy milk
1 teaspoon apple cider vinegar
½ cup vegan butter
¾ cup granulated sugar
½ cup dark brown sugar, firmly
    packed
5 ripe, medium-sized bananas
1 tablespoon vanilla extract
6 tablespoons dark rum

SALTED CARAMEL FROSTING:

1 cup vegan butter
3½ cups confectioners' sugar
⅓ cup dark brown sugar, firmly
    packed
½ teaspoon salt
1½ teaspoons water
1 teaspoon vanilla extract

SAUTÉED BANANAS:

2 tablespoons dark brown sugar,
    firmly packed
1 tablespoon dark rum
1 firm, large banana, sliced into
    ¼-inch rounds

Preheat your oven to 350°F (175°C) and lightly grease and flour two 8-inch round cake pans.

In a small bowl, whisk together the flour, baking powder, baking soda, and salt, and set aside. In a separate small bowl, combine the nondairy milk and vinegar, also moving this to the side for now.

In your stand mixer, cream together the butter and both sugars until light and fluffy. Mash the bananas well and mix them in, along with the vanilla. Add the flour mixture, alternating with the milk in two or three additions, into your mixer. Ensure that everything is fully combined before equally dividing the batter between your two prepared pans.

Bake for 25 to 30 minutes, until a toothpick inserted into the center of each layer comes out clean. Remove from the oven, and while they are still warm, poke the cake tops numerous times with your testing toothpick. Pour 3 tablespoons of rum over each layer. Let the cake layers cool completely before turning them out of the pans to assemble.

For the frosting, cream the butter well and incorporate the confectioners' sugar slowly. Microwave the brown sugar, salt, and water together for 30 to 60 seconds, just until the sugar dissolves and begins to bubble a bit. Let the brown sugar stand for a few minutes to cool off, then pour it into the butter mixture. With the mixer on high, beat the frosting vigorously

(continued on next page)

until all the ingredients are fully incorporated, light, and fluffy. Stir in the vanilla and frost the cake as desired.

For the final banana garnish, combine the brown sugar and rum in a non-stick skillet over medium heat. Cook until the sugar dissolves. Add the banana slices and stir to coat all the pieces well. Sauté for about 2 minutes, until the sugar bubbles and darkens into a golden caramel, stirring gently every so often. Remove the bananas from the skillet and transfer them to a silicone baking mat. Separate each slice so that they do not stick together. Let them cool completely before applying them artistically to adorn the cake.

Caramel Macchiato Cheesecake

Makes 12 to 16 servings

Coffee runs through my veins, an essential that is unequaled for its power to both stimulate and sustain. The scent of a fresh roast percolating on the counter is enough to brighten my whole day, restorative and comforting, yet still incredibly complex. Each cup is an enigma. Thus, black coffee is my go-to, despite the vast array of syrups and drizzles and sprinkles that proliferate on café menus. Caramel macchiato is the one big exception that tempts me as a special reward, or a serious boost on a particularly difficult day. Aromatic as a buzzy coffee shop, dressed up with a sour cream substitute for crema and signature crosshatched caramel, now you can have your coffee and eat it, too.

CHOCOLATE COOKIE CRUST:

1½ cups Chocolate Wafer Cookie (page 229) crumbs
¼ cup vegan butter or coconut oil, melted
¼ teaspoon salt

COFFEE CHEESECAKE:

1 (12-ounce) package extra-firm silken tofu
2 (8-ounce) packages vegan cream cheese
⅔ cup granulated sugar
2 tablespoons instant coffee powder
¼ cup coffee liqueur
1 teaspoon vanilla extract
⅛ teaspoon salt

VANILLA SOUR-CREMA TOPPING:

1 cup vegan sour cream
1 tablespoon vanilla extract
¼ cup granulated sugar
1 tablespoon cornstarch

Preheat your oven to 350°F (175°C) and lightly grease a 9-inch springform pan.

For the crust, place the cookie crumbs in a medium bowl and pour the melted butter or coconut oil on top. Add the salt, stirring to thoroughly coat all the crumbs, and transfer this mixture into your prepared pan. Use your palms to firmly press the crumbs down, taking care to completely cover the bottom in an even layer. Bake for approximately 10 minutes and let cool but leave the oven on.

For the main body of the cake, drain the package of tofu before tossing it into your food processor or blender to puree. Once smooth, add in the cream cheese and sugar, processing again to combine. In a small dish, stir the coffee powder into the liqueur to dissolve all the granules. Add this mixture into your food processor or blender, and process to combine. Add the vanilla and salt, scrape the sides to make sure you are not leaving anything out of the mix, and process one last time. Pour the mixture into your pan and tap gently on a flat surface to release any air bubbles trapped below the surface. Smooth down the top with a spatula and bake for 20 minutes. After that time, lower the oven temperature to 325°F (160°C). Bake for an additional 20 to 25 minutes, until the cake is still a bit wobbly in the center but set around the edges and slightly darker in color.

As the cake finishes baking, stir together the sour cream, vanilla, sugar, and cornstarch in a small bowl until smooth. Once the

(continued on page 109)

CARAMEL SAUCE:

¼ cup vegan butter

⅔ cup coconut sugar or dark brown sugar, firmly packed

2 tablespoon unsweetened non-dairy milk

¼ teaspoon salt

4 teaspoons cornstarch

cake comes out of the oven, pour this mixture over the top, and smooth it down to achieve an even layer. Bake for 5 to 10 minutes more, just until bubbles begin to percolate around the edges. The cake will still seem rather loose and wobbly, but it will continue to set up as it cools. Let it cool to room temperature before making the caramel drizzle.

To complete the cake, make the caramel sauce by first setting a saucepan on the stove and gently melt the butter over medium heat. Once liquefied, add in the sugar, nondairy milk, and salt. Whisking slowly and steadily, bring the mixture to a gentle boil and continue to cook for about 5 minutes. Stir in the cornstarch and whisk vigorously to prevent lumps. Cook for one more minute, remove from the heat, and let the sauce cool for at least 10 minutes before drizzling over the cake in a checkerboard pattern, or as desired.

Chai Cheesecake

Makes 12 to 16 servings

The spicy nuances of chai tea are no longer the stuff of obscure exotic imports alone, but is still shamefully hard to come by in prepared sweets. Those that do attempt such a delicate balance typically play it safe with milder mixes that lean heavily on cinnamon as a crutch, creating a terribly watered-down tease. Skip the middleman, start from scratch, and you seize upon the true, piquant flavors of chai without diluting your dessert. Each dense slice sparkles with a heavy dose of real ground spices that impart an intense experience, sure to please even the most discriminating chai enthusiasts.

GRAHAM CRACKER CRUST:

1½ cups graham cracker crumbs
¼ cup vegan butter or coconut oil, melted
1–2 tablespoons plain nondairy milk

CHAI FILLING:

1 (12-ounce) package extra-firm silken tofu
2 (8-ounce) packages vegan cream cheese
1 cup granulated sugar
2 teaspoons ground ginger
1½ teaspoons ground coriander
1 teaspoon ground cinnamon
½ teaspoon ground allspice
½ teaspoon cardamom
¼ teaspoon ground cloves
¼ teaspoon ground black pepper
Dash salt

Preheat your oven to 375ºF (190ºC) degrees and lightly grease and flour a 9-inch round springform pan.

Toss the graham cracker crumbs into a medium bowl. Add the melted butter or coconut oil and stir to combine. Slowly drizzle in the nondairy milk, just a few teaspoons at a time, until the crumbs are moist enough to hold together when pressed, but not so much that they're damp. Using your hands, press the mixture evenly into the bottom of your prepared pan. Set aside.

For the filling, drain the tofu of any excess water and blend it in your food processor or blender until smooth. Add in the cream cheese and blend. Scrape down the sides and blend again, ensuring that no lumps remain. Incorporate the sugar, spices, and salt. Scrape down the sides once more, checking for any concentrated pockets of spice. Blend thoroughly to create a homogenous mixture before pouring it on top of your graham cracker crust. Tap the whole pan on the counter lightly, to even it out and eliminate any air bubbles. Smooth the top with your spatula before transferring it to the oven. Bake for approximately 30 minutes, until the sides begin to pull away from the pan and the center still appears to be rather wobbly when tapped. Trust me; it will become firmer in time!

Let the cake cool completely before moving it into the refrigerator, where I suggest you let it chill for at least 12 to 24 hours before serving. This will allow the flavors to fully develop and intensify.

Cookies and Crème Pound Cake

Makes 10 to 12 servings

Statistically speaking, the Oreo® has ranked as America's favorite cookie for decades, or at least for as long as market researchers have peered into the snacking habits of the country. Yet, for all its nostalgic, unfussy charm, the simple stacked wafers might pale in comparison to a plateful of cake. Choosing between the two would be some sort of cruel trial, a war of wills I'd never force anyone to undergo. Peace is possible, if you bake it! Get the best of both with a thick slab of moist pound cake, riddled with crunchy cookie pieces all the way through. Don't call it a compromise; it would pull in top honors if added to the survey.

POUND CAKE:

¼ cup vegan butter

¾ cup granulated sugar

1½ cups all-purpose flour

1 teaspoon baking powder

½ teaspoon baking soda

½ teaspoon salt

½ cup plain or unsweetened vegan yogurt

½ cup plain nondairy milk

1 teaspoon vanilla extract

½ teaspoon apple cider vinegar

1 cup crushed vegan chocolate crème-filled sandwich cookies (about 10 whole cookies)

4 whole vegan chocolate crème-filled sandwich cookies

Preheat your oven to 350ºF (175ºC) and lightly grease an 8x4-inch loaf pan.

Using your stand mixer, cream together the butter and granulated sugar. Add in the flour, baking powder, baking soda, salt, and yogurt all at once. Mix until just combined but be careful not to overwork the batter; a few lumps are okay at this point. Proceed by mixing in the nondairy milk, followed by the vanilla and vinegar. Fold in your crushed cookies by hand and pour the batter into your prepared loaf pan. Place the remaining whole cookies on top, and bake for 40 to 50 minutes, until a toothpick inserted into the center of your loaf comes out clean.

Let the cake cool in the pan for at least 5 minutes before unmolding and moving it to a wire rack.

Cool completely, slice, and enjoy with a tall glass of soy milk, just like the classic cookie!

Cranberry Red Velvet Cake

Makes 10 to 14 servings

What's made with cocoa but doesn't taste like chocolate, and is a brilliant ruby-red hue but has no added food coloring? If you said red velvet cake, then you sure do know your desserts! Something of a pop culture sleeper hit, the red velvet cake is said to have originated from wartime scarcity, a humble confection made of the most basic staples that just happened to turn red due to the strange alchemy between natural cocoa powder and baking soda. Most renditions rely instead on some artificial augmentation, but with a little bit of baking know-how and an eye toward natural alternatives, it's easy to stack up layers of any shade, no questionable additives needed.

Taking advantage of the naturally red fruit, cranberries lend both their subtle coloring and bold, tart, and tangy flavor to the batter, dotting the finished cake with chewy bites of whole stewed cranberries. No red velvet creation is complete without a bit of cream cheese frosting, and this vanilla-infused topper is the perfect sweet foil to such an unconventional cake. Denser and darker than the standard crumb, just a sliver will satisfy any craving, but you still may just find yourself reaching for seconds nonetheless. If you're looking to revamp the classic dessert offerings at your next celebration, consider your search complete.

CRANBERRY RED VELVET CAKE:

- 2½ cups cranberries, fresh or frozen
- ¼ cup light brown sugar, firmly packed
- 2 tablespoons lemon juice
- ¼ cup finely diced, steamed beet (about 1 small beet)
- ⅔ cup olive oil
- ⅔ cup unsweetened nondairy milk
- ¼ cup beet juice
- 1½ teaspoons vanilla extract
- 1 teaspoon apple cider vinegar
- 2⅓ cups all-purpose flour
- 1⅓ cup granulated sugar
- ¼ cup natural cocoa powder*
- 1½ teaspoons baking powder
- ½ teaspoon salt
- ⅛ teaspoon ground cinnamon

Preheat your oven to 350°F and lightly grease and flour two 8-inch round cake pans.

Combine the cranberries, brown sugar, and lemon juice in a medium saucepan over moderate heat. Stir periodically and allow the mixture to stew for 10 to 15 minutes, roughly mashing the cranberries against the side of the pan to help thicken the mixture. Once it reaches a jammy consistency, thick enough to coat the back of a spoon, turn off the heat and let cool for at least 15 minutes.

In the meantime, toss the cooked beet, oil, nondairy milk, beet juice, vanilla, and vinegar into your blender and puree on high speed. Blend until completely smooth, pausing to scrape down the sides of the canister if needed.

In a separate large bowl, whisk together the flour, granulated sugar, cocoa powder, baking powder, salt, and cinnamon. Make sure that all the dry goods are equally distributed within the bowl before adding in all of the blended wet ingredients along with the stewed cranberries. Stir with a large spatula to bring everything together into a smooth batter, being careful not to overmix. A few remaining lumps are just fine.

(continued on next page)

CREAM CHEESE FROSTING:

2 (8-ounce) packages vegan cream cheese
1 cup vegan butter, at room temperature
5 cups confectioners' sugar
1 teaspoon vanilla extract
Pinch of salt

Distribute the batter equally between the two prepared cake pans and tent the pans loosely with foil to prevent the tops from browning. Bake for 28 to 32 minutes, until a toothpick inserted into the centers pulls out cleanly. Let cool completely before frosting.

To prepare the frosting, simply combine the vegan cream cheese and butter in your stand mixer with the whisk attachment installed. Beat the two together thoroughly until smooth and homogenous before adding in half of the confectioners' sugar with the vanilla and salt. Start the mixer on a low speed to incorporate the sugar, pausing to scrape down the sides of the bowl with your spatula. Add in the remaining sugar in the same fashion, giving the mixer plenty of time to blend it in. Turn up the speed to high and whip the frosting for a full 5 to 10 minutes, until light and fluffy. Apply to your cake as desired.

Because this frosting is fairly soft, it's advisable to store the finished cake in the fridge just prior to serving if you want to make it in advance.

*Using natural cocoa is very important for maintaining color integrity; do not use Dutch-process cocoa powder in this recipe if you want the crumb to remain red.

Dark Mocha Revelation Cake

Makes 10 to 12 servings

Stealing top honors at my very first baking competition, the stunning success of this imposing ode to chocolate and coffee may be responsible for the obsession with recipe creation that soon took hold. Emboldened by this early success, I was gripped by renewed inspiration before even wrapping my hands around the award, continuing to tweak the prizewinner until not a soul could resist its charm. It is intensely flavored and highly aromatic. Simply leaving it uncovered on the counter will draw curious noses from all over the house, in search of the heavenly aroma. Dense and decadent, this cake should only be made for a crowd, lest you find yourself compelled by its siren song to polish the whole thing off unassisted!

MOCHA CAKE:

2 cups all-purpose flour
½ cup Dutch-process cocoa powder
1 tablespoon baking powder
1 teaspoon baking soda
½ teaspoon salt
1 (14-ounce) can chickpeas, drained
1¼ cups maple syrup
1 cup olive oil
1 cup chocolate nondairy milk
2 teaspoons instant coffee powder
1 tablespoon vanilla extract

COFFEE BUTTERCREAM:

½ cup vegan butter
2 cups confectioners' sugar
1 tablespoon vanilla extract
2 tablespoons unsweetened
    nondairy milk
2½ teaspoons instant coffee powder
½ cup dark chocolate-covered
    espresso beans

CHOCOLATE COATING:

⅔ cup full-fat coconut milk
½ cup vegan butter
10 ounces (about 1⅔ cups) dark
    chocolate, chopped
1 cup dark chocolate-covered
    espresso beans

Preheat your oven to 325°F (160°C) and lightly oil and flour two 8-inch round cake pans.

Sift the flour, cocoa powder, baking powder, baking soda, and salt into your stand mixer and set aside. Drain any excess liquid out of the canned chickpeas before tossing them into your food processor or blender and pureeing until completely smooth. Scrape down the sides to ensure that no pieces are left behind, and add in the maple syrup and oil, processing just to combine. Add these wet ingredients into the dry. Blend briefly, just to incorporate.

In a separate microwave-safe bowl, heat the nondairy milk in the microwave for just a minute and dissolve the coffee powder into it. Add this mixture, along with the vanilla, into the batter, stirring to fully combine. Divide the batter evenly between your prepared pans and smooth down the tops. Bake for 30 minutes, until the cakes appear to pull away from the sides slightly. Give the cakes time to cool completely off before proceeding.

To make the buttercream, simply blend all the ingredients, except for the espresso beans, in your mixer until smooth and creamy. Roughly crush the ½ cup of espresso beans and set them aside.

When you are ready to assemble the cake, turn the first layer out onto the plate you want to serve it on. Mound your buttercream up high but in an even layer, using all of it. Sprinkle the crushed espresso beans on top, covering the entire area of exposed filling.

(continued on page 119)

Next, take the second layer and flip it onto the base with the flat side up, resulting in a smooth surface on top.

Finally, heat the coconut milk and butter together in the microwave for one minute, or until the butter melts. Place the dark chocolate in a medium bowl and hot liquid mixture on top. Let it sit for about a minute to start melting before stirring vigorously to combine. If it doesn't all smooth out after a good deal of stirring, send it all to the microwave for 30 seconds or so to help it along. Let this smooth ganache sit and thicken for up to an hour at room temperature, or for 15 to 25 minutes in the refrigerator. Smooth the ganache over the top of the cake and down the sides. Crush the remaining 1 cup of espresso beans and apply them in an even layer around the edges, to coat the sides of the cake before the ganache has fully set. Serve this cake within 24 hours to enjoy the flavors and textures at the peak of perfection.

Chocolate-covered espresso beans made without dairy can be hard to come by, but you can still experience the same crunchy, caffeinated crumb to coat this cake with a simple shortcut. Coarsely grind ¼ cup of dark roasted coffee beans with 1½ cups finely chopped dark chocolate. The resulting mix may not have the same shine, or compulsive snackablility, but it's every bit as an invigorating and satisfying as a garnish!

Everyday Almond Cake

Makes 10 to 12 servings

This moist, fine-crumbed cake was originally created for a birthday celebration, fulfilling the vague request for something featuring almonds and chocolate. Delivering a truly decadent double decker tower on the day of the event, little did I know what fame and glory lay ahead of this sweet smash hit. Rapidly evolving into a single, daintier round fit for a bite of indulgence any day of the week, it became a staple at Nourish Café, where I baked in San Francisco for almost two years. Now one of my signature desserts, it's simpler to whip together on a whim, dare I say "healthier," and still every bit as delicious. Hundreds of cakes later, I can confidently say that it will not disappoint on any occasion.

ALMOND CAKE:

½ cup almond meal
¾ cup white whole wheat flour
½ cup garbanzo bean flour
½ teaspoon baking powder
½ teaspoon baking soda
¼ teaspoon salt
⅓ cup olive oil
1 cup plain nondairy milk
½ cup + 2 tablespoons maple
   syrup
½ teaspoon apple cider vinegar
1½ teaspoons almond extract
½ teaspoon vanilla extract

CHOCOLATE GANACHE:

7 ounces (about 1 heaping cup)
   dark chocolate, chopped
¼ cup full-fat coconut milk
1 tablespoon maple syrup
Whole almonds, for garnish
   (optional)

Preheat your oven to 350°F (175°C) and generously grease one 8-inch round cake pan.

Combine the almond meal, both flours, baking powder, baking soda, and salt. Stir to combine and set aside.

Separately, whisk together the oil, nondairy milk, maple syrup, and vinegar vigorously until the mixture is slightly frothy and bubbly on the surface. Incorporate the two extracts. Slowly add in the dry mixture, whisking just until everything is combined. Don't be alarmed if the batter seems thin, almost like crepe batter rather than your traditional cake. That means you've done it right!

Pour the batter into your prepared pan and bake for 25 to 35 minutes, until a toothpick inserted into the center comes out clean. Let cool for at least 15 minutes before turning out on a wire rack to cool. Make sure it's completely cool before decorating.

To make your ganache, heat the chocolate, coconut milk, and maple syrup together in a medium saucepan over very low heat, stirring well until completely smooth. Pour generously over the top of the cake, allowing it to run down the sides. Use a flat spatula to smooth over any gaps until it's fully covered. Place whole almonds decoratively around the border, if desired. Let the ganache cool and set completely before serving.

If you'd still like to enjoy the original, "decadent" rendition, simply double the recipes for both the cake and ganache, and create a double-decker layer cake by sandwiching extra ganache between the two rounds.

Lemon-Lime Sunshine Bundt

Makes 16 to 18 servings

When you're stuck inside on gloomy days, cloudy skies threatening overhead, take shelter in the kitchen and brighten the mood with a slice of this cheerful cake. Tangy fresh citrus like lemons and limes make me think of bright colors, bubbly sodas, and hot summer days. Using them in a dessert such as this is just like baking sunshine into a cake! Go off the beaten path and play with any variety of zesty fruit, like orange, grapefruit, yuzu, pomelo, Buddha's hand, and more to shake up the usual routine.

LEMON-LIME CAKE:

¾ cup plain nondairy milk
2 tablespoons lemon juice
2 tablespoons lime juice
1 cup vegan butter
2 cups granulated sugar
2 tablespoons lemon zest
2 tablespoons lime zest
1¼ cups lemon, lime, or plain
    vegan yogurt
3 cups all-purpose flour
2 teaspoons baking powder
½ teaspoon baking soda
½ teaspoon salt

GLAZE:

½ cup confectioners' sugar
1–2 tablespoons lemon juice

Preheat your oven to 325°F (160°C) and lightly grease and flour a 10-inch Bundt or tube pan.

In a small bowl, combine the nondairy milk with both citrus juices and set aside to acidify.

In a stand mixer, cream the butter, sugar, and both zests together until light and fluffy, scraping down the sides as necessary. Add in the yogurt, a heaping ½ cup at a time, beating well after each addition to prevent unblended lumps from being left behind.

In a separate bowl, combine the flour, baking powder, baking soda, and salt. Add these dry ingredients into your stand mixer alternately with the acidified milk mixture. Mix thoroughly.

Drop dollops of the batter evenly into your prepared Bundt pan and bake for 65 to 80 minutes, until a toothpick inserted into the center comes out clean. Let the cake cool in the pan for 10 minutes before turning it out onto a wire rack. Allow it to cool completely before icing.

For the glaze, simply whisk the sugar and lemon juice together until smooth and pour over your cake as desired.

Prefer smaller format sweets? Turn your sweet edible sunshine into individual cupcakes by dividing the batter equally between 18–20 standard muffin pans lined with cupcake papers. Bake at 350°F (175°C) for 15–18 minutes.

Ispahan is the unique combination of raspberry, lychee, and rose originally dreamed up as a specialty macaron by legendary pastry chef Pierre Hermé. Take a page from his notebook and incorporate 1 teaspoon of rosewater into the cakes to enjoy this exquisite delicacy.

Lychee Cupcakes with Raspberry Frosting

Makes 13 cupcakes

Lychees are not an everyday produce pick but are worth hunting down. Fragrant and delicately flavored like exotic flowers and subtly grassy herbs, pureed lychees give these cupcakes a distinctive, inimitable taste. Capped with a swirl of soft raspberry frosting, the tart berry twang enhances the flavors locked within each tender, moist crumb.

Fresh lychees are always best. You can find them proliferating in Asian markets around late spring and through summer, but if you still have no luck finding them, canned lychees will work in a pinch.

LYCHEE CUPCAKES:

¾ pound fresh lychee nuts (roughly 7 ounces of puree)

¾ cup granulated sugar

⅓ cup olive oil

¼ teaspoon vanilla extract

1¼ cups all-purpose flour

½ teaspoon baking powder

¾ teaspoon baking soda

¼ teaspoon salt

½ teaspoon apple cider vinegar

RASPBERRY FROSTING:

½ cup vegan butter

½ cup vegan cream cheese

6 ounces (about 1 cup) fresh raspberries

4 cups confectioners' sugar

Before breaking out those cupcake pans, you will want to peel, pit, and process the lychees first. To do so, press your thumb into the top of the fruit, as you would an orange, and remove the outer skin. The fruit itself is a translucent white color; split in half to remove the pit. Toss the pure flesh into your food processor or blender and repeat with your remaining lychees. If they are being stubborn, you can always take a knife all the way around the circumference to remove the inedible exterior. Once you have taken care of the lychees, process them until mostly smooth and set aside.

Preheat your oven to 350°F (175°C) and line twelve to thirteen muffin tins with cupcake papers.

In a large bowl, mix together the lychee puree, sugar, oil, and vanilla until completely combined. Next, sift in the flour, baking powder, baking soda, and salt, stirring just enough to bring the batter together, but being careful not to overmix. Finally, once your oven is ready to go, stir in the apple cider vinegar. Spoon the batter into your prepared tins about ½ to ⅔ of the way to the top. Though you may be able to squeeze the batter into twelve tins, I typically end up with a perfect baker's dozen. Bake for 15 to 17 minutes, until evenly browned and a toothpick inserted into the center of a cupcake, comes out clean. Let the cupcakes cool completely before frosting.

For the frosting, cream together the butter and cream cheese in your stand mixer. Make sure you wash and dry your berries well before proceeding. Set aside 13 of the nicest berries for garnish. Throw the rest of the raspberries into your food processor or blender and blend them until completely smooth. Pass the puree through a fine-mesh strainer and discard the solids. Pour the seedless blend into your stand mixer and beat until everything is mostly incorporated. Mix in 2 cups of the confectioners' sugar. Once the first batch of sugar has combined, add the remaining 2 cups. Start mixing on slow, just to incorporate, and then bring the speed up to high, whipping for about 5 minutes until the frosting is light and fluffy. Pipe or spread the frosting onto your cupcakes as desired, and top with the reserved berries.

Marshmallow Mud Cake

Makes 10 to 12 servings

Billowing swells of puffy white clouds of pure vanilla delicacy are what childhood dreams are made of. Marshmallow cream, soft and airy, seems like an unthinkable fluke of nature, genuine proof of magic, for its unworldly loft and sweetness. Call upon your inner wizard to conjure up a burgeoning, puffy bowlful with only a few common household ingredients, plus a little pinch of sweet sorcery. The devilishly dark chocolate cake lurking underneath such an angelic, sweet topping is an alchemical wonder to behold all by itself, but a true marvel to partake in combination.

CHOCOLATE CAKE:

¾ cup chocolate nondairy milk
½ cup Dutch-process cocoa powder
1 teaspoon apple cider vinegar
¼ cup vegan butter
¼ cup dark brown sugar, firmly packed
½ cup granulated sugar
1 teaspoon vanilla extract
2 tablespoons olive oil
1 cup all-purpose flour
1 teaspoon baking soda
¼ teaspoon salt

MARSHMALLOW TOPPING:

⅓ cup aquafaba, chilled
¾ cup granulated sugar
½ teaspoon cream of tartar
⅛ teaspoon xanthan gum
½ teaspoon vanilla extract

CHOCOLATE ICING:

1 tablespoon vegan butter
½ cup confectioners' sugar
1 tablespoon Dutch-process cocoa powder
1 tablespoon water

Preheat your oven to 350ºF (175ºC) and lightly grease an 8-inch round cake pan.

In a microwave-safe bowl, heat the nondairy milk for about 2 minutes on high so that it just begins to boil. Stir in the cocoa powder, making sure it has completely dissolved before stirring in the vinegar. Set aside to cool.

Use your stand mixer to cream together the butter, both sugars, and the vanilla. Scrape down the sides and add in the oil, beating well to combine. Beat in the cooled cocoa mixture. Sift in the flour, baking soda, and salt, mixing until everything is just incorporated.

Pour the batter into your prepared pan and spread it down into an even layer. Don't worry if it seems like a skimpy amount of batter; it rises a bit in baking, and the marshmallow topping compensates for any lack of height! Bake for 18 to 22 minutes, until a toothpick inserted into the center of the cake comes out clean. Let it cool completely before removing from the pan.

To make the marshmallow topping, place the aquafaba in the bowl of your stand mixer with the whisk attachment installed. Beginning on low, beat the aquafaba until a light froth forms before increasing the speed to medium. Meanwhile, whisk together the sugar, cream of tartar, and xanthan gum in a small bowl, ensuring that all the ingredients are thoroughly distributed before proceeding. With the motor still running, slowly sprinkle in this dry mixture just a little bit at a time, until it's all incorporated. Increase the speed to high and continue to whip for 8–10 minutes. The sugar should have dissolved so it no longer appears grainy, and the aquafaba should be bright white, glossy, and fluffy, with peaks firm enough to stand on their own. Gently fold in the vanilla last. Spread liberally over the cake.

For the final chocolate flourish, simply melt the butter and whisk in the confectioners' sugar, cocoa, and water until smooth. Pour this icing over your cake as desired, or use it as a sauce to serve on the side.

Mini Icebox Cheesecake

Makes 3 to 4 servings

For me, sweets are a perennial consideration, but the hot weather and humidity of summer can be a powerful deterrent to turning on the oven. Fortunately, not all desserts need to be baked, as is the case with this creamy little cake made to beat the heat. Much like an ice cream cake in consistency but with the pleasant tang of cream cheese, it is the best adaptation of a cheesecake under the sun, if I dare say so myself. Plus, unlike the large commitment of standard, full cheesecakes, this one is perfectly sized for an intimate party between a few close friends!

Should you prefer a more generous cake to accommodate the appetites of a bigger party, double the recipe and use a 9-inch springform pan instead. It will be slightly taller than the small version, but I can't imagine anyone will complain about receiving larger slices.

GRAHAM CRACKER CRUST:

1 cup graham cracker crumbs
3 tablespoons vegan butter
2 tablespoons maple syrup

MARBLED CHEESECAKE FILLING:

1 (8-ounce) package vegan cream cheese
⅓ cup granulated sugar
2 tablespoons plain nondairy milk
1 tablespoon lemon juice
2 teaspoons vanilla extract

FRUIT TOPPING:

½ cup strawberry jam or preserves
1 teaspoon water

Place the graham cracker crumbs in a medium bowl. Melt the butter and pour it over the crumbs, followed by the maple syrup. Mix to coat and moisten all the crumbs before pressing the mixture firmly into a 6-inch round springform pan, covering the bottom in one even layer. Chill it in the freezer while you assemble the filling.

Blend the cream cheese, sugar, nondairy milk, lemon juice, and vanilla in a food processor or blender until the mixture is completely smooth and creamy. Remove the crust from the freezer and pour the filling carefully inside.

For the final flourish, mix together the jam or preserves with the water in a small bowl. Spoon it on top and mix very lightly with a spatula to swirl it throughout.

Cover the cake with plastic wrap and return it to the freezer for at least 5 hours, until set and sliceable.

Any other flavor of jam, from cherry to apricot, would be right at home here, but don't overlook alternative seasonal spreads, like apple or pumpkin butter, too.

Not-Nog Cupcakes

Makes 24 cupcakes

Paging through a Christmas kitchenware catalog during the holiday season, one recipe in particular caught my eye: eggnog bread. As one might expect from a mainstream publication at that time, the dense loaf was saturated with mind-boggling measures of eggs, milk, butter, and of course eggnog. Converting this into an unlikely vegan variant was a challenge I simply could not turn down! A failed batch and many crafty adjustments later, the original quick bread had morphed into cupcakes, and my kitchen was filled with a veritable elf's workshop of lightly spiced, very merry holiday gifts. The resulting recipe comfortably fed a sizable holiday party, as it does make a whole lot of little cakes, but I wouldn't recommend reducing the batch. . . . Leftovers are unlikely with any crowd.

NOG CUPCAKES:

1½ cups vegan butter

2 cups granulated sugar

1½ teaspoons ground nutmeg

½ teaspoon vanilla extract

½ teaspoon kala namak (black salt)

1 tablespoon ground flaxseeds

2 tablespoons water

3¾ cups all-purpose flour

2 teaspoons baking powder

½ teaspoon baking soda

2 cups vegan eggnog, store-bought or homemade (page 233)

BUTTERED RUM GLAZE:

½ cup vegan butter

1 cup dark brown sugar, firmly packed

¼ cup vegan eggnog

2 tablespoons dark rum

¼ teaspoon salt

4 cups confectioners' sugar

½–1 cup sliced almonds, for garnish

Preheat your oven to 350°F (175°C) and line two dozen muffin tins with cupcake papers.

In your stand mixer, cream the butter with the sugar, nutmeg, vanilla, and black salt. While the mixer churns, blend the flaxseeds with the water, allowing them to sit and slightly gel. Introduce the flax mixture into the bowl of the stand mixer and stir to combine. The batter will be somewhat lumpy at this point, but as long as you don't have any obscenely large clumps of solid butter, it should be fine.

In a separate bowl, combine your flour, baking powder, and baking soda. Slowly add these dry ingredients to the contents of the bowl waiting in your stand mixer, alternating with the eggnog until both are used up. Fully incorporate each addition but be careful not to overmix.

Pour the resulting batter into your prepared cupcake liners about ⅔ to ¾ of the way full and bake for 20 to 22 minutes. The cupcakes should not appear particularly browned; keep a close eye on them. They will be done when a toothpick inserted into the center of a cake comes out clean.

For the glaze, place the butter and brown sugar in a medium saucepan over medium heat. Stir until the butter melts and the sugar dissolves, creating a smooth syrup. Add the eggnog, rum, and salt, and bring the mixture to a gentle boil. Remove from the heat. Slowly introduce the confectioners' sugar, whisking vigorously into the mixture until the glaze thickens and loses a little of its shine; 1 to 2 minutes. Pour or spoon a dollop on top of each cupcake. Garnish with sliced almonds, lavishing your little cakes with as much of the nuts as desired.

Orange Dreamsicle Snack Cake

Makes 9 to 12 servings

Any kid who's ever chased after the siren song of an ice cream truck undoubtedly has fond memories of those classic, creamy orange ice pops, quickly melting under the summer sun. Turning the nostalgic combination of sweet citrus and rich vanilla into a tender, compulsively snackable sheet cake is not only a fun new take on the frozen dessert, but an improvement on the original; you won't need to worry about making a drippy, sticky mess, no matter how high the temperatures climb!

SNACK CAKE:

3½ cups all-purpose flour
1 cup granulated sugar
1 teaspoon baking soda
½ teaspoon baking powder
½ teaspoon salt
⅔ cup vanilla or plain vegan yogurt
¼ cup olive oil
1 tablespoon vanilla extract
1 cup orange juice

DREAMSICLE TOPPING:

½ cup vanilla or plain vegan yogurt
1 cup confectioners' sugar
2½ tablespoons tapioca starch
    or 1½ tablespoons arrowroot
    powder
1 teaspoon vanilla extract
½ cup orange marmalade, store-
    bought or homemade (page 239)

Preheat your oven to 350°F (175°C) and lightly grease a 9x13-inch baking pan.

Combine the flour, sugar, baking soda, baking powder, and salt in a medium bowl and set aside. In a stand mixer, whisk together the yogurt and oil until fully emulsified. Add in the vanilla and orange juice. Slowly incorporate the dry ingredients in stages, until the batter is nicely mixed without lumps. Pour the batter into your prepared pan.

For the topping, whisk together the yogurt, confectioners' sugar, starch or arrowroot, and vanilla in a small dish, stirring until smooth. Drizzle over the batter. Microwave the marmalade for about 30 seconds, until slightly liquefied and easier to pour. Drizzle it over the batter as well. Swirl both toppings together with a knife but try not to overdo it as you may muddle the colors.

Bake for 25 to 30 minutes, until a toothpick inserted into the center of the cake comes out clean. When testing for doneness, be sure to find a spot that is free from topping, as the icing and marmalade may cause the toothpick to appear wet, even if the cake is ready. Wait until the cake has cooled completely before cutting into bars.

> If **strawberry shortcake bars** were more your jam while growing up, simply swap out the marmalade for strawberry preserves and add ½ cup crispy brown rice cereal over the top of the batter after swirling, for a slightly crunchy finish.

Peach Melba Layer Cake

Makes 10 to 14 servings

As the story goes, the original peach melba was created for a famous opera singer who loved ice cream but did not dare eat it for fear of paralyzing her vocal cords. A brilliant chef thought to pair the forbidden frozen treat with poached peaches and a raspberry sauce, hoping the added elements might lessen the chill. While I can't claim to understand either of these theories, I do know that a timeless dessert was born that night. That said, if the chef had really been thinking on his feet, he might have cut the icy interloper out entirely to make an unassailable layer cake. Hold the ice cream this one time, and enjoy a warmer embrace from this fruity diva.

PEACH CAKE:

2 pounds sliced and pitted
    peaches, fresh or frozen and
    thawed
½ cup olive oil
1 cup granulated sugar
⅓ cup coconut sugar or dark brown
    sugar, firmly packed
1 tablespoon lemon juice
2½ cups all-purpose flour
2 teaspoons baking powder
1½ teaspoons baking soda
½ teaspoon ground ginger
½ teaspoon salt

VANILLA FROSTING:

1½ cups vegan butter
4 cups confectioners' sugar
1 tablespoon vanilla extract
2 tablespoons unsweetened non-
    dairy milk

RASPBERRY FILLING:

1 (12-ounce) jar raspberry jam
    (about 1½ cups)
1 cup fresh raspberries, for garnish
    (optional)

Preheat your oven to 350°F (175°C) and generously grease and flour two 8-inch round cake pans.

Place the peach slices in your food processor or blender, breaking down the fruit into a mostly smooth puree, but leave a few chunks of fruit to add texture to the cake. Set aside.

In a large bowl, whisk together the oil and both sugars until light and fluffy. Add in your peach puree along with the lemon juice and mix to combine. In a separate bowl, sift together the flour, baking powder, baking soda, ginger, and salt. Slowly add these dry ingredients into your bowl of liquids and stir until everything is incorporated. Equally divide the batter between your two prepared pans. Bake for 25 to 30 minutes, until a toothpick inserted into the center of each layer comes out clean. Cool completely.

For the vanilla frosting, simply blend all the frosting ingredients together with a mixer, starting at a low speed so that the sugar does not fly out. Once the ingredients have adequately combined, whip the frosting on a higher speed for at least 3 minutes, to add more air and lighten it a bit.

When you are ready to assemble the cake, turn both layers out of the pans and slice each in half horizontally, creating four round layers total. Use a sawing motion with a serrated knife to achieve a clean cut, and be very careful when moving the layers to avoid crumbling. Lay the first bottom down on the platter you intend to serve it on, and spread it with a third of the raspberry jam.

(continued on next page)

To prevent the two fillings from mingling, drop a generous dollop of the vanilla frosting in the very center of the layer (atop the jam) and smooth it down and out to the edges. Put the other unfrosted half of the cake layer on a separate plate and use it to place this layer neatly on top of the nicely spread filling. Frost the top of this one in the same manner. Repeat the frosting process with the remaining two layers until you reach the top. Skip the raspberry jam on the very top and simply decorate with vanilla frosting and fresh raspberries, if desired.

Perfect Lemon Poppy Seed Cupcakes

Makes 12 cupcakes

Whoever first discovered that flavors as seemingly mismatched as lemon and poppy seeds could be successfully united in sweet harmony was one brilliant lunatic. My only quibble with this combination is that these distinctive components each deserve more time in the spotlight. A crazy proposition to be sure, but by sequestering the poppy seeds in the cake and giving the lemon plenty of room to shine in a jammy eggless filling, both have equal opportunities to bask in the spotlight.

LEMON CURD:

½ cup instant mashed potato flakes

½ cup plain nondairy milk

2 tablespoons vegan butter

¼ cup lemon juice

½ cup granulated sugar

1 tablespoon lemon zest

¼ teaspoon turmeric

POPPY SEED VANILLA CUPCAKES:

1 cup plain nondairy milk

1 teaspoon apple cider vinegar

1 cup all-purpose flour

¼ teaspoon baking powder

1 teaspoon baking soda

½ teaspoon salt

¼ cup olive oil

½ cup granulated sugar

1½ tablespoons poppy seeds

1 tablespoon vanilla extract

To make the lemon curd, combine the potato flakes and nondairy milk in a microwave-safe bowl. Heat for about 30 seconds until the starchy flakes absorb all the liquid. Stir in the butter, allowing it to melt in the residual heat. Mix in the lemon juice and sugar. Heat the mixture again in the microwave for another 30 to 45 seconds until it reaches a consistency much like applesauce. Toss it into your food processor or blender along with the lemon zest and turmeric, and puree for 2 or 3 minutes, until it is completely smooth and creamy. Refrigerate the resulting curd for at least 4 hours before using, or better yet, let it sit overnight so that it has time to thicken and intensify in flavor.

With the curd prepared and chilled, it is time to make the cupcakes! Preheat your oven to 350ºF (175ºC) and line a dozen muffin tins with cupcake papers.

In a small bowl, whisk together the nondairy milk and vinegar and let it rest for 5 minutes. Meanwhile, sift the flour, baking powder, baking soda, and salt into a medium bowl, and set aside. Blend the oil and sugar together, followed by the slightly curdled milk, and beat the mixture for a minute, forming a loose matrix of bubbles. Slowly add in the dry ingredients, stirring the batter just enough to combine, being careful not to overmix. Finally, fold in the poppy seeds and vanilla. This makes a very thin, delicate batter; do not panic if it seems watery.

Pour the batter into your prepared muffin tins, until it reaches about ¾ of the way to the top of the liners. Bake for 17 to 20 minutes, until a toothpick inserted into the center of a cupcake

(continued on page 139)

comes out clean. Let the cupcakes cool for 10 minutes in the tins before removing them to a wire rack, where they should cool completely.

Describing how to assemble the cupcakes can get a bit wordy and sound intimidating, but it will be much easier once you try it for yourself. First off, get your cupcakes and take the lemon curd out of your refrigerator. Take the first cupcake and insert a paring knife at the very edge of the top at an approximately 45-degree angle. Run the blade around the entire circumference at this angle, until the top pops off and you have a little cone of cake. Cut the excess triangle of cake away from the top that you just removed, so that the bottom is smooth. This remaining triangle isn't used for anything else, so go ahead and treat yourself to a snack! Now, take the flat top and press a small, sharp cookie cutter into it. You want to use a shape that leaves a good amount of space around the border so that it doesn't tear. (Oh, and you can eat the cutout, too. Who knew this recipe would be so rewarding for the baker?)

Next, take a spoonful of the lemon curd and drop it into the hollow in the base of the cake, smoothing it out so that it comes right up to the top. Replace the cut cupcake top and voilà—edible art! Just be careful when handling them because they have a bit less structural integrity than standard, solid cupcakes.

Piña Colada Mini Bundts

Makes 6 mini Bundts

Picture yourself lying in the sun, sand between your toes, parrots crooning overhead. Not a worry in the world, you have everything you need: sunblock, a good companion, and a refreshing tropical drink. You reach over to take another sip, when you realize that it is not a drink at all, but a tiny cake! In fact, it is then that you realize you are not on the beach, but at home in your kitchen, with a freshly baked batch of these amazing mini Bundt cakes! Even if your immediate surroundings are cold and gray, you can still have a taste of the sweet life with these unique tropical delights.

PIÑA COLADA CAKE:

1½ cups unsweetened shredded coconut, toasted and divided
¼ cup coconut oil, melted
⅓ cup granulated sugar
2 tablespoons coconut sugar or dark brown sugar, firmly packed
1 cup crushed pineapple, drained
1 cup all-purpose flour
1 teaspoon baking powder
¼ teaspoon salt
¾ cup full-fat coconut milk
2 tablespoons dark rum
1 teaspoon lime juice

GLAZE:

1 cup confectioners' sugar
1 tablespoon unsweetened shredded coconut
2–3 tablespoons dark rum

> Go big or just go Hawaii, already! Double the recipe and bake in a full-sized Bundt pan with a 12-cup capacity if you're in dire need of a seriously sweet escape. Allow 60 to 75 minutes for the cake to bake all the way through.

Preheat your oven to 350ºF (175ºC) and lightly grease a mini Bundt pan or a jumbo muffin pan.

Toss 1 cup of the toasted coconut into your food processor and grind it down into a fine powdery consistency. It may take about 5 minutes, but when you see the coconut starting to clump together, you're good to go. If you do not have a food processor handy, then whiz the coconut in a spice grinder in batches of ¼ to ½ cup, depending upon the capacity of your appliance.

Place the powdered coconut into a large bowl along with the melted coconut oil and both sugars. Thoroughly mix everything together. Drain any excess liquid from the crushed pineapple, add it to the mixture, and combine. Sift in the flour, baking powder, and salt and mix once more. Stir in the remaining toasted coconut, coconut milk, rum, and lime juice, stirring just until incorporated. It's fine to leave a few errant lumps behind.

Pour the batter into your prepared pans and bake for 30 to 35 minutes, until a toothpick inserted into the center of a cake comes out clean. Let the cakes rest in their pans for 10 minutes before transferring them to a wire rack. Allow them to cool completely before icing.

For the glaze, simply whisk the sugar together with the shredded coconut and as much rum as necessary to achieve your desired thickness and color. Err on the side of less rum for more distinctive, solid stripes, or more for lighter, more complete coverage. Drizzle over the little cakes and enjoy a taste of the tropics, no matter your locale!

It's cool to be square, too. This cake can alternately take shape in a lightly greased 9-inch square pan. Simply bake at 325°F (160°C) for about 90 minutes to ensure that it's fully and evenly cooked through the center.

Plum-Good Crumb Cake

Makes 10 to 12 servings

Crumb cake, alternately known in some circles merely as "coffee cake," is understandably popular around teatime, with a pinch of spice, a good bit of sugar, and that irresistible topping. Aficionados can agree that the crumb topping is the best part, which is why this rendition doubles down on the buttery streusel for a particularly generous helping. While alone this would secure its place next to a steaming hot cuppa, the ribbon of juicy fresh plums through the center seals the deal. If plums don't make the cut in your fruit basket, try another fruit, or a combination, such as peaches, apples, or pears. No matter what you tuck into the center, the outcome will still be plum good.

CRUMB TOPPING:

1 cup all-purpose flour
½ cup coconut sugar or dark brown
    sugar, firmly packed
1½ teaspoons ground cinnamon
⅛ teaspoon ground cardamom
½ teaspoon salt
6 tablespoons vegan butter or
    coconut oil

CAKE:

½ cup plain nondairy milk
½ teaspoon apple cider vinegar
½ cup vegan butter
1 cup granulated sugar
2 cups all-purpose flour
1 teaspoon baking powder
¾ teaspoon baking soda
½ teaspoon salt
1½ cups plain vegan yogurt
1 teaspoon vanilla extract

FRUIT FILLING:

¾ pound (3–4 medium) fresh
    plums, pitted and chopped
1 tablespoon all-purpose flour

Preheat your oven to 350ºF (175ºC) and lightly grease a 10-inch tube pan or Bundt pan.

For the crumb topping, whisk together the flour, sugar, cinnamon, cardamom, and salt in a medium bowl. Melt the butter or coconut oil and pour it over the dry ingredients. Stir with a fork to coat everything evenly, forming coarse crumbs in various sizes. Set aside.

For the cake, combine the nondairy milk and vinegar in a medium bowl and whisk together. Let this sit for a few minutes to curdle. Separately, cream the butter and sugar together in a stand mixer, beating for a few minutes to fully combine. Sift the flour, baking powder, baking soda, and salt into a separate bowl. Add the yogurt and vanilla to your curdled milk. Add the dry ingredients into the stand mixer, alternating with the wet while beating on low speed. Occasionally scrape down the sides to make sure you do not leave any large lumps behind. Be careful not to overmix, as it is okay to leave a few small lumps in the batter.

As you are about to assemble the cake for baking, toss the chopped plums with a tablespoon of flour. Pour half of your batter into the prepared pan, spreading it to coat the bottom in an even layer. Sprinkle the fruit over the first layer of batter. Follow this with the remaining half of your batter, being careful to completely cover all the fruit. Sprinkle the crumb mixture over the top before sliding the pan into the oven. Bake for 50 to 60 minutes, until a toothpick or skewer inserted into the center of the cake comes out clean. Let cool completely in the pan prior to serving.

Pomegranates can be fickle fruits, messy and difficult to work with—unless you know the secret to easily removing the arils. Slice off the crown and score the sphere into six equal wedges. Gently pry the segments apart. Working with one piece at a time, submerge each in a bowl of water and use your fingers to loosen the arils from the membrane. The edible seeds will sink to the bottom, while the membrane will float. When you're all done, simply pour off the water along with all the pith. You should now have a bowl of nothing but the sweet, tart, tangy arils, ready to eat!

Pomegranate Ginger Cupcakes

Makes 12 cupcakes

Pomegranate briefly enjoyed a flash of viral fame, trending right alongside kale and the other superfoods du jour, but this jewel box of curiously tart, tangy, and sweet gems will earn genuine staying power in your home once you try these fragrant cupcakes. With a double dose of the ruby red juice to intensify the typically delicate flavor, the only thing that could possibly make them better is the sharp but sweet bite of ginger. Much more sophisticated than your average kiddie cupcakes, these will delight the adventurous palate seeking more than just a yellow cake with gaudy rainbow sprinkles.

CUPCAKES:

2 cups 100% pomegranate juice, divided
1 teaspoon apple cider vinegar
¾ cup granulated sugar
⅓ cup olive oil
1 teaspoon vanilla extract
1½ cups + 1 tablespoon all-purpose flour, divided
½ teaspoon baking powder
½ teaspoon baking soda
¼ teaspoon salt
¼ cup crystallized ginger, finely minced
1½ teaspoons lemon zest

GINGER FROSTING:

½ cup vegan butter
2 cups confectioners' sugar
2 teaspoons ground ginger
1 teaspoon vanilla extract
1–2 tablespoons unsweetened nondairy milk
¼ cup fresh pomegranate arils, for garnish (optional)

In a small saucepan over medium heat, cook 1 cup of the juice for about 20 minutes, until it is reduced to a little less than ¼ cup. Remove from the heat and let cool.

Preheat your oven to 350ºF (175ºC) and line one dozen muffin tins with cupcake papers.

Combine the remaining cup of pomegranate juice and the vinegar in a medium bowl, leaving them alone for a few minutes to get acquainted. Mix the juice vigorously until frothy, and whisk in the sugar, oil, and vanilla. Sift in the flour, baking powder, baking soda, and salt, and stir just until combined. Toss the minced ginger with the remaining 1 tablespoon of flour, and fold both the ginger and zest into your batter.

Divide the batter evenly among the cupcake papers, and drizzle equal amounts of your reserved pomegranate reduction over each cupcake just before baking. Bake for 18 to 22 minutes, until lightly browned, and a toothpick inserted into the center of a cupcake comes out clean. Let the cupcakes cool inside the muffin tins for about 15 minutes, before moving them to a wire rack. Allow them to cool completely before frosting.

In a medium bowl, combine all the ingredients for the frosting, and whip until smooth and fluffy. Frost your heart out! Top with fresh pomegranate arils if desired.

Pup Cakes

Makes 2 small or 1 medium cake

Dogs are just as important as any other member of the family, so whenever a canine birthday comes up, cake is still a mandatory component of the celebration. This particular treat was inspired by my very first four-legged best friend, Isis. It was her favorite surprise snack, judging by the way she inhaled it; in mere minutes the entire thing would be reduced to a few errant crumbs, which she would inevitably vacuum up in short order as well! Now the newest addition to my furry family, Luka, is quite a bit smaller and pickier than the old lady, so I've adapted this doggie delight into a more compact, crowd-pleasing format. You can even enjoy this cake with your lucky pup, since it is made with ingredients that are also perfectly agreeable to the human palate. Think of it as a dense peanut butter carrot cake, if you will. If you are still a beginner baker, then this is the perfect recipe to start with, as I am certain that your dog will be your most easily pleased critic!

¼ cup spelt or whole wheat flour
¼ teaspoon baking powder
¼ cup shredded carrots
1 tablespoon creamy peanut butter
1 tablespoon coconut oil, melted
2 tablespoons unsweetened
    applesauce
¼ teaspoon apple cider vinegar
2 tablespoons plain, unsweetened
    vegan yogurt

Preheat your oven to 350°F (175°C) and lightly grease 2 wells of a muffin tin or 1 medium 6-ounce ramekin.

Combine the flour and baking powder in a medium bowl. Stir in the carrot shreds and then incorporate the peanut butter, melted coconut oil, applesauce, and vinegar, and mix well. The batter will be very thick, much like cookie dough. Divide the batter between the muffin tins or drop it all into your ramekin. Bake for 25 to 35 minutes, until a toothpick inserted into the center comes out clean. Let cool completely.

Right before serving, spread the yogurt on top to act as a creamy, healthy frosting. Stand back and watch your fur baby gobble it up!

Root Beer Float Cupcakes

Makes 12 cupcakes

When I was too young to reach the top shelf of the fridge, and my parents still exercised the authority to regulate my intake of sweets, I remember the harshest restrictions were placed upon soda. It was only once a year, on New Year's Eve, that I would be allowed a glass of the fizzy elixir. If I was really lucky, I was permitted a scoop of ice cream and some chocolate syrup to make a root beer float. Memories of these rare celebratory moments were the inspiration for this cupcake. Root beer is infused into the little cakes, which are topped with a more grown-up chocolate ganache, and dense vanilla frosting reminiscent of that cool scoop of ice cream. Elevated beyond the specter of a midnight snack but still playful at heart, it's still one of my most popular recipes to this day.

ROOT BEER CUPCAKES:

1 cup root beer soda

1 teaspoon apple cider vinegar

⅔ cup granulated sugar

⅓ cup olive oil

½ teaspoon vanilla extract

2 teaspoons root beer extract (available online if you can't find it)

1⅓ cups all-purpose flour

½ teaspoon baking powder

¾ teaspoon baking soda

⅛ teaspoon salt

CHOCOLATE GANACHE:

3 ounces (½ cup) semi-sweet chocolate chips

2 tablespoons plain non-dairy milk

1 teaspoon maple syrup

VANILLA FROSTING:

1 cup vegan butter

3 cups confectioners' sugar

2 teaspoons vanilla extract

Preheat your oven to 350ºF (175ºC) and line a dozen muffin tins with cupcake papers.

In a large bowl, combine the soda and vinegar and let stand for a few minutes. Add in the sugar, oil, and both extracts, whisking vigorously until slightly frothy. In a separate bowl, combine the flour, baking powder, baking soda, and salt. Gently pour the liquid mixture into the bowl of dry ingredients, stirring with a wide spatula to incorporate. A few lumps are fine to leave in the batter; be careful not to overmix.

Distribute the batter evenly between the prepared tins, filling the cupcake liners approximately ¾ of the way to the top. Bake for 18 to 22 minutes, until a toothpick inserted into the center of a cupcake comes out clean. After letting the cupcakes cool in the pans for about 10 minutes, move them to a wire rack and allow them to cool completely before preparing the ganache.

When the cupcakes are ready, combine all the ingredients for the ganache in a microwave-safe container and microwave for about 60 seconds. Stir thoroughly to help incorporate the melting chocolate. If the chocolate is not yet entirely smooth, return the sauce to the microwave for 15 to 30 second intervals, stirring between each heating, watching carefully to ensure that it doesn't burn. Drizzle the ganache in squiggles over the tops of the cupcakes. Allow to fully cool and dry before preparing the frosting.

With your stand mixer, beat the vegan butter thoroughly to soften. Add in the confectioners' sugar, and beat on a low speed, so as not to spray powder everywhere. Incorporate the vanilla, and whip on high speed for 5 to 6 minutes, until the frosting is thick and creamy. Apply to your cupcakes as desired and enjoy.

Self-Frosting Peanut Butter Cupcakes

Makes 12 cupcakes

Okay, you got me. These treats are not going to pick up a knife all on their own and smear a nice dollop of frosting all over themselves. However, they do come out of the oven fully dressed and ready to devour! The trick is to swirl in a thick spoonful of the peanut buttery cocoa spread before baking them, and presto, your work is all done the instant the timer goes off! Now, if only layer cakes were so self-sufficient . . .

PEANUT BUTTER CUPCAKES:

⅔ cup plain nondairy milk

1 teaspoon apple cider vinegar

½ cup granulated sugar

½ cup coconut sugar or dark brown sugar, firmly packed

2 tablespoons whole flaxseeds

¼ cup water

½ cup creamy peanut butter

½ cup unsweetened applesauce

½ teaspoon vanilla extract

1½ cups all-purpose flour

1 teaspoon baking powder

½ teaspoon baking soda

½ teaspoon salt

CHOCOLATE-PEANUT BUTTER FROSTING:

½ cup creamy peanut butter

¼ cup Dutch-process cocoa powder

⅔ cup confectioners' sugar

¼ cup plain nondairy milk

Preheat your oven to 350ºF (175ºC) and line one dozen muffin tins with cupcake papers.

In a large bowl, combine the nondairy milk and vinegar, and let sit for a few minutes before whisking vigorously until frothy. Mix in both sugars. Grind the flaxseeds into a powder with a spice grinder before blending them together with the water. Stir the flaxseeds mixture, peanut butter, applesauce, and vanilla into the bowl, and beat until thoroughly combined. In a separate bowl, add the flour, baking powder, baking soda, and salt. Slowly stir these dry ingredients into the batter. Mix until there are no more lumps, but be careful not to mix more than necessary.

In a separate bowl, combine all the ingredients for the frosting, and stir until completely smooth.

Divide your batter equally between the prepared muffin tins. Drop a dollop of frosting into each cup of raw batter, and swirl it around with a toothpick, covering the entire top. Bake for 20 to 25 minutes, until a toothpick inserted into a cupcake comes out clean. When testing for doneness, be sure to find a spot that is free from frosting, as it may cause the toothpick to appear wet, even if the cupcakes are ready. Let the cupcakes cool inside the tins for at least 10 to 15 minutes. You can either let them cool the rest of the way atop a wire rack, or serve them immediately for a warm delight!

Silken Chocolate Mousse Cake

Makes 12 to 16 servings

If love can be compared to chocolate, then consider this cake to be an intense and steamy affair with the seductive tempt-ress next door. Perched atop a soft, no-bake almond crust is a mousse so luxurious, velvety, and thick that a fork could remain upright in a slice without assistance. Topped off with a scandalous veil of chocolate curls, this alluring little number is hard to resist. Once you have indulged in this deep, dark hedonistic pleasure, you may never be able to go back to a plain-Jane chocolate bar ever again.

COCOA-ALMOND BASE:

1½ cups almond meal
⅓ cup Dutch-process cocoa
    powder
¼ cup maple syrup
3 tablespoons coconut oil, melted

CHOCOLATE MOUSSE:

2 (12-ounce) packages extra-firm
    silken tofu
½ cup Dutch-process cocoa
    powder
¾ cup granulated sugar
1 tablespoon vanilla extract
⅛ teaspoon salt
12 ounces (about 2 cups) semi-
    sweet chocolate chips
1 bar dark chocolate (optional,
    for garnish)
Lightly grease the bottom of a
    9-inch round springform pan.

In a small bowl, combine all the ingredients for the base and mix well, until a moist but firm dough forms. Drop the dough into the center of the springform pan and press firmly so that it evenly covers the bottom. It helps if you start by easing the dough out with your fingertips, but to get a nice edge when you reach the sides, simply press the crust in with the bottom of a measuring cup. Once you have the bottom nicely covered, let the crust chill in the refrigerator while you prepare the filling.

First, drain any excess liquid away from your tofu before tossing it into your food processor or blender. Puree thoroughly and add in the cocoa, sugar, vanilla, and salt, pulsing briefly to incorporate. Place the chocolate in a microwave-safe dish, and microwave in 30-second intervals to prevent scorching. Stir thoroughly after each heating until the chocolate is completely melted. Continue stirring to achieve a very smooth consistency. Pour the melted chocolate into your waiting tofu mixture. Blend once more for about 2 or 3 minutes, pausing as needed to scrape down the sides to achieve a completely smooth, homogenous mixture.

Pour the filling into your chilled base and use a spatula to smooth the top to the best of your ability. The mousse is quite thick and therefore difficult to smooth, but you will be covering up the top with more chocolate anyway! Return your springform pan to the refrigerator and allow the cake to chill for at least 3 hours.

When you are ready to serve, take a vegetable peeler to the short side of the chocolate bar and shave off thin pieces to adorn the top. It's easiest to form curls if the bar is at room temperature or just slightly warmer; colder, and it will break into shorter flakes or shards.

Triple-Threat Chocolate Cheesecake

Makes 12 to 16 servings

Calling all chocoholics! This is the dessert you've been waiting for. You don't need to be an obsessive fan of all things cacao to appreciate such a showstopper, though. No one in their right mind would be able to refuse this three-layer skyscraper of cheesecake, increasing in chocolate intensity as you dig in deeper. When you have picky guests to please, stack the deck in your favor with this ace in your pocket. I swear, it's not cheating, just an easy win!

COCOA CRUST:

1½ cups vegan graham cracker crumbs

⅓ cup confectioners' sugar

¼ cup Dutch-process cocoa powder

¼ cup vegan butter

CHEESECAKE:

1 (12-ounce) package extra-firm silken tofu

3 (8-ounce) packages vegan cream cheese

¾ cup granulated sugar

1 tablespoon vanilla extract

¼ teaspoon salt

12 ounces (2 cups) semi-sweet chocolate chips

GANACHE:

¾–1 ounce (about 2 tablespoons) semi-sweet chocolate chips

½ teaspoon olive oil

Preheat your oven to 350°F (175°C).

For the crust, stir together the graham cracker crumbs, confectioners' sugar, and cocoa powder in a medium bowl. Melt the butter and incorporate it into the dry ingredients, forming a crumbly but moist mixture. Use your hands to press this mixture into the bottom of a 9-inch round springform pan. Set aside.

For the filling, drain the tofu of any excess water and blend it in a food processor or blender until smooth. Add in the cream cheese, blend, and scrape down the sides with a spatula. Blend again, ensuring that no lumps remain. Integrate the sugar, vanilla, and salt. Place the 2 cups of chocolate chips in a large microwave-safe bowl, and microwave in 30-second intervals to prevent scorching. Stir thoroughly after each heating until the chocolate is completely melted. Continue stirring to achieve a very smooth consistency.

Remove 1½ cups of the cheesy filling and thoroughly blend it into the chocolate. From this mixture, remove 2 cups and spread it evenly atop the crust. Remove 1½ additional cups of the cheese mixture and blend it into the chocolate mixture. Remove 2 more cups of the resulting mixture and gently spread it over the first chocolate cheesecake layer. Finally, stir the rest of the cheese filling into the remaining chocolate mixture. Carefully pour and spread this final batch of chocolate mixture over the previous two layers. Work very gently, as the top layers are less solid and more likely to combine. If it happens, don't worry; it will still taste just as good!

Smooth out the top and bake for 50 to 55 minutes. The sides will not pull away from the pan, so you will just have to trust your intuition on this one. After removing it from the oven, use a knife to immediately loosen the cake from the sides, but leave it inside the pan and allow it to cool to room temperature.

To make the ganache, microwave the remaining 2 tablespoons of chocolate chips with the oil until melted and completely smooth, about 30 to 60 seconds. Stir together and drizzle over top of the cake. Refrigerate the cake for at least 12 hours before serving.

Wasabi Chocolate Cupcakes

Makes 12 cupcakes

Don't let their innocent appearance fool you; these are no bland baby cakes. Lurking deep within the heart of each paper-wrapped chocolate morsel is a potent dose of peppery wasabi, surprising the unprepared with a serious punch of heat. Wasabi can be extremely powerful even in small quantities, so don't underestimate the meager-looking amounts suggested here without a glass or two of nondairy milk on hand to fight the flames. Ramp it up or dial it down according to taste, but if you choose to tempt fate and add in more, don't say I didn't warn you!

WASABI CHOCOLATE CUPCAKES:

1½ cups all-purpose flour
½ cup Dutch-process cocoa powder
1 cup granulated sugar
1 teaspoon baking powder
1 teaspoon baking soda
½ teaspoon salt
½ cup olive oil
1 cup plain nondairy milk
1½–2 teaspoons wasabi paste
½ cup dark or semisweet chocolate chips
2 teaspoons apple cider vinegar

WASABI ICING:

½ teaspoon wasabi paste
3 tablespoons plain nondairy milk
1 cup confectioners' sugar

Preheat your oven to 350°F (175°C) and line one dozen muffin tins with cupcake papers.

Begin by mixing the flour, cocoa powder, sugar, baking powder, baking soda, and salt in a medium bowl. Combine the oil, nondairy milk, and wasabi paste in a separate bowl. Beat until the wasabi is fully dissolved and the mixture is slightly frothy. Slowly add your wet ingredients to the bowl of dry ingredients and stir until everything is just combined. Be careful not to overmix, as a few lumps are okay. Gently fold in the chocolate chips. Finally, add the vinegar and quickly stir it in.

It may look like more batter than will fit into just one dozen muffin cups but go ahead and fill the papers most of the way to the top, and immediately slide the tins into the oven. Bake for 18 to 20 minutes, until a toothpick inserted into the center of a cupcake comes out clean. Allow the cupcakes to cool in the pans for at least a few minutes before removing them to a wire rack.

For the icing, whisk the wasabi and nondairy milk together in a small bowl, ensuring that no lumps of wasabi are left. Add the confectioners' sugar and whisk until smooth. Drizzle the glaze sparingly over the cupcakes.

PIES & TARTS

Baklava Tart

Makes 8 to 14 servings

Tired of finicky phyllo? Heartbroken over honey? No matter, you can still make a modified baklava that will compete with the best of them. Originally created as a way to use up remnants of phyllo after a little pastry mishap, the phyllo is merely crumbled over the top; no careful layering is necessary to produce an impressive dessert. The amount of pastry sprinkled on top is very imprecise, allowing a lot of wiggle room to use however much you want. If there aren't any open packages of phyllo dough on hand just waiting to be used up, you can purchase the mini frozen shells and only crush up as many as necessary, thereby reducing waste. Now, isn't that a delicious fix!

CRUST:

3½ ounces (¼ cup + 2 tablespoons)
    vegan cream cheese
¼ cup granulated sugar
¼ cup dark brown sugar, firmly
    packed, or coconut sugar
1 teaspoon vanilla extract
1 teaspoon lemon juice
1 tablespoon light agave nectar or
    maple syrup
1½ cups all-purpose flour
¼ teaspoon baking soda
¼ teaspoon salt

NUTTY FILLING:

2 cups chopped walnuts
⅓ cup granulated sugar
1 tablespoon ground cinnamon
¼ teaspoon salt
¼ cup vegan butter or coconut oil,
    melted
3½–4 ounces (¼ of a package, or
    8–10 frozen mini shells) phyllo
    dough scraps

GLAZE:

2 tablespoons vegan butter or
    coconut oil
⅓ cup light agave nectar or maple
    syrup
1 tablespoon dark brown sugar,
    firmly packed, or coconut sugar
½ teaspoon lemon juice
½ teaspoon vanilla extract

Preheat your oven to 350°F (175°C) and lightly grease a 13x4-inch rectangular tart pan with a removable bottom. While I like how this shape mimics that of a slice of traditional baklava, a 9-inch round fluted tart pan with removable bottom could also be used.

For the crust, blend together the cream cheese and both sugars in your stand mixer, creaming until well combined. Stir in the vanilla, lemon, and agave or maple syrup. Add in 1 cup of the flour, the baking soda, and salt, and mix until fully incorporated. Add the remaining ½ cup of flour and mix well. Press the resulting mixture into your prepared tart pan, bringing it evenly and smoothly up the sides. Dock the crust by pricking the bottom all over with a fork, creating vents for steam to escape and preventing big bubbles from getting trapped inside. Bake for 15 to 17 minutes, until lightly golden brown in color. Remove the pan from your oven but leave the heat on.

In a medium bowl, stir together the walnut pieces, sugar, cinnamon, and salt. Pour the melted butter or coconut oil over everything in the bowl, stirring to coat. Gently press the nut mixture into the crust so that it fits in an even layer. Crumble enough phyllo over the top to cover the nuts completely. Return the pan to the oven, and bake for an additional 20 to 22 minutes, until the phyllo becomes nicely browned.

After removing your tart from the oven, melt the final measure of butter for the glaze in a small bowl. Stir in all the remaining ingredients and pour this mixture evenly over the top of your tart while it is still warm. This will help bind everything together and sweeten the tart a bit more. Let the tart cool for at least two hours before slicing.

Berry Froyo Chiffon Pie

Makes 8 to 10 servings

A beauty to behold and a charmer on the lips, the real secret to this fluffy frozen pie is how laughably easy it is to whip up. If you've ever stood in a kitchen, even only once in your life, I think you could manage this recipe with aplomb. Plus, since it's based on yogurt and jam, I would feel entirely justified slicing off a generous wedge for dessert or even breakfast or lunch alike.

As the seasons change, this same formula can be adapted to suit your shifting cravings on demand. One of my favorite variations is swapping in vanilla yogurt for the base while swirling pumpkin or apple butter (page 227) instead of jam, effortlessly complementing any winter holiday feast.

GRAHAM CRACKER CRUST:
- 1½ cup graham cracker crumbs (from about 12 full rectangle sheets)
- 6 tablespoons vegan butter or coconut oil, melted

BERRY FROYO FILLING:
- 1 (14-ounce) can full-fat coconut milk, chilled
- ½ cup confectioners' sugar
- ½ cup strawberry vegan yogurt
- ½ cup blueberry vegan yogurt
- ½ cup raspberry jam or preserves

TO SERVE (OPTIONAL):
- Whipped Coconut Cream (page 243)
- Fresh berries

To make the crust, break up the graham crackers into smaller pieces before pulsing in a food processor until very finely ground. The resulting crumbs should be about the consistency of coarse almond meal. Pick out any larger pieces and reprocess as needed.

Drizzle the melted butter or coconut oil into the crumbs, stirring thoroughly to moisten the ground cookies. The mixture should be capable of sticking together when pressed.

Transfer the mix to a 9-inch round pie pan and use lightly moistened fingers to firmly press it down on the bottom and along the sides. Use the bottom of a flat measuring cup or drinking glass for smoother edges.

Carefully open the chilled can of coconut milk, being sure not to shake it, and scoop off the top layer of thick coconut cream that will have risen to the top. Save the watery liquid left behind for another recipe, such as a soup or a curry. Place the coconut cream in the bowl of your stand mixer and install the whisk attachment. Whip on high speed for about 3 minutes before slowly beginning to sprinkle in the sugar, just a little bit at a time. Continue beating the mixture for up to 10 minutes, until light and fluffy.

In a separate bowl, combine both yogurts and stir in a dollop of the Whipped Coconut Cream. This will help lighten up the mixture to make it easier to blend in the rest. Once fully incorporated, add the remainder of the Whipped Coconut

Cream, folding gently with a large spatula until well-blended. Be careful to stir gently so as not to knock all the bubbles out of the airy, whipped mixture.

Add in the jam or preserves last, mixing just enough to incorporate but leaving it well marbled throughout the filling. Spoon into your prepared crust, smooth over the top, and move the whole pie into your freezer. Let rest until solidified; at least 4 to 6 hours, but ideally 8 to 12.

To serve, simply slice the pie into wedges and top with additional dollops of Whipped Coconut Cream and fresh berries, if desired.

Cashew Crème Pear Tart

Makes 8 to 10 servings

Imagine delicately spiced pears cooked until just fork tender, sitting atop a luscious pillow of maple-scented cashew crème, all contained within a soft, nutty crust. Sound like a dream? Well wake up, because this delight is easily a reality! This is one amazing finish to any meal, sure to please all palates and diets alike. Not only is it gluten-free, utilizing almond flour and cornmeal for an unconventional press-in-pan crust, but this tart can also be adapted for low-sugar diets. Simply omit the granulated sugar in the pear topping and crust with more almond meal. The only danger of serving a dessert suitable for all stripes of eaters is that everyone will want more than just one serving! You might be wise to save yourself a slice before presenting this grand finale to a crowd, as the likelihood of leftovers by the end of the night will be slim to none.

CRUST:

¼ cup granulated sugar or coconut
    sugar
1 cup almond flour or almond meal
¼ cup yellow cornmeal
¼ cup chickpea flour
1/8 teaspoon salt
¼ cup vegan butter or coconut oil
1–2 tablespoons water

CASHEW CRÈME:

1½ cups raw cashews, soaked for
    4–6 hours and drained
⅓ cup plain nondairy milk
¼ cup maple syrup
1 teaspoon vanilla extract

PEAR TOPPING:

2 firm, medium-sized pears
¼ cup granulated sugar
½ teaspoon ground cinnamon
¼ cup sliced almonds, for garnish

Preheat your oven to 325ºF (160ºC).

Combine the sugar, almond flour or meal, cornmeal, chickpea flour, and salt in a medium bowl. Melt the butter or coconut oil and pour it in, along with the water. Stir to combine all the dry ingredients and press this mixture firmly into a lightly greased 9-inch round tart pan with a removable bottom. Bake for 10 minutes and let cool, leaving the oven on.

In a blender or food processor, begin blending the soaked cashews, nondairy milk, maple syrup, and vanilla. Once the nuts are mostly broken down, crank up your machine to high speed and thoroughly puree. It may take 5 to 10 minutes for the mixture to become completely smooth, so don't stop short. Pause as needed to scrape down sides of the container with your spatula to ensure that there are no lumps. Smooth the resulting crème into your crust and set aside.

Peel, core, and thinly slice the pears. Toss the slices with the sugar and cinnamon to evenly coat. Arrange them in an overlapping spiral on top of the cashew crème layer. Bake for 20 to 25 minutes, until the pears are fork-tender. Let cool and sprinkle with sliced almonds before serving.

Any leftover pear slices that don't quite fit on top of your tart shouldn't be destined for the compost, but could top a thick slice of toast! Bake them in any small oven-safe dish for 10 to 15 minutes until fork tender. Let cool for a few minutes before piling on top of a buttered slice of toast, and enjoy for snack or breakfast. If you want to get real fancy, go all out and slather it with cream cheese first and top it with chopped hazelnuts.

Cherry Cola Pudding Pie

Makes 10 to 12 servings

A drink menu without cola is not only a theoretical abomination, but an apparent impossibility. No matter the cuisine, clientele, or locale, every bar and restaurant seem to have some version of the unmistakable yet indescribable sparkling elixir. In fact, it's so popular that some regions simply refer to all soft drinks simply as "cola," rather than "soda" or even "pop." Some err more on the side of crisp and tart citrus, while others lean heavily on warm vanilla and cinnamon, although you'd never know such a range of nuances exist based on the limited mainstream options. Two brands continue to dominate the immense market so despite its universal availability, cola creativity falls flat. Think outside the bottle with an injection of fruit and tart cherry sweetness in this refreshing pudding pie.

GRAHAM CRACKER CRUST:
1½ cups graham cracker crumbs
5 tablespoons vegan butter or
    coconut oil, melted

CHERRY COLA FILLING:
1½ cups cola soda
½ cup 100% cherry juice
1 cup unsweetened nondairy milk
¼ cup arrowroot powder
2½ teaspoons agar powder
½ teaspoon vanilla extract
⅛ teaspoon salt

TO GARNISH:
Whipped Coconut Cream
    (page 243)
Fresh cherries

Wishing you could have an old-fashioned float in a more contemporary format? Skip the whipped cream and top slices with scoops of No-Churn Vanilla Bean Ice Cream (page 237) instead. Consider your wish granted!

For the best texture, be sure to pulse your graham crackers in a food processor until very finely ground. The resulting crumbs should be about the consistency of coarse almond meal. Pick out any larger pieces and reprocess as needed.

Drizzle the melted butter or coconut oil into the crumbs and stir thoroughly. The mixture shouldn't be quite damp, but moist, and capable of sticking together when pressed.

Transfer the mix to a 9-inch round pie pan, using lightly dampened fingers to firmly press it down on the bottom and along the sides. Use the bottom of a flat measuring cup or glass for smoother edges. Place the crust in your fridge to set.

Next, prepare the cherry cola filling. Combine everything in a medium saucepan, thoroughly whisking to make sure there are no lumps of starch remaining. Heat over a moderate flame, stirring occasionally, just until it comes to a boil. Turn off the heat and pour the hot pudding into your prepared piecrust, tapping it gently on the counter to smooth out the top. Return the pie to the fridge and chill for at least 6 hours for the filling to be firm enough to slice.

Just prior to serving, pipe or dollop the coconut whipped cream around the border as artfully or generously as you desire, and finish with fresh cherries on top.

Chili Chocolate Tart

Makes 12 to 14 servings

Albeit a cinch to make and equally effortless to serve, the very first bite will reveal that this is no quotidian chocolate tart. With a kick of spice and the satisfying crunch of pecans, the myriad flavors and textures will entertain your palate well beyond the obligatory, ordinary chocolate dessert. Try serving this rich but modestly sweetened tart with a dollop of Whipped Coconut Cream (page 243) or No-Churn Vanilla Bean Ice Cream (page 237) to contrast the intense and spicy flavors.

CANDIED PECANS:

3 tablespoon dark brown sugar, firmly packed, or coconut sugar
1½ cups pecan halves
1 teaspoon ground cinnamon
¼ teaspoon ground cayenne pepper
¼ teaspoon salt
1 tablespoon vegan butter or coconut oil

CHOCOLATE CRUST:

1½ cups Chocolate Wafer Cookie (page 229) crumbs
1 teaspoon ground cinnamon
¼ teaspoon salt
½ cup vegan butter or coconut oil

CHOCOLATE FILLING:

8 ounces dark chocolate, finely chopped
½ teaspoon ground cinnamon
½ teaspoon smoked paprika
¼–½ teaspoon ground cayenne pepper
¼ teaspoon salt
1 cup full-fat coconut milk
¼ cup vegan butter or coconut oil
¼ teaspoon almond extract
1 teaspoon vanilla extract

GARNISH (OPTIONAL):

¼ teaspoon crushed red pepper flakes
¼ teaspoon flaky sea salt

Preheat your oven to 350ºF (175ºC) and line a baking sheet with a silicone baking mat or parchment paper.

In a medium bowl, toss together the sugar, pecans, cinnamon, cayenne, and salt. Melt the butter or coconut oil and pour it over the nut mixture, tossing to evenly coat. Spread the pecans in one even layer on your prepared baking sheet. Bake for about 10 minutes, keeping a close eye on them, being very careful not to cook them for too long. By the time the pecans start to look dark brown or smell nutty, they are probably already burnt. Once removed from the oven, immediately transfer the pecans to a fresh sheet of parchment paper, shake off any excess glaze, and separate any that are touching. Let the pecans cool but leave the oven on.

For the crust, combine the cookie crumbs, cinnamon, and salt in a medium bowl. Melt the butter or coconut oil and pour it in, stirring to form a moist but crumbly mixture. Press this into a 9-inch round tart pan with a removable bottom. Bake for 20 minutes, until dry to the touch, and set aside.

To make the filling, place the chocolate, spices, and salt in a large bowl. Separately, begin heating the coconut milk in a small saucepan over medium heat. Add the butter or coconut oil into the saucepan, stirring until melted. Bring the mixture just to the brink of boiling, then immediately pour it into the bowl containing your chocolate. Let everything sit for a couple of minutes, and then stir vigorously to melt the chocolate and form a completely smooth mixture. As the chocolate cools, add in both extracts. Pour the chocolate mixture into your prepared crust and tap lightly on the counter to remove any air bubbles. Let it sit for 15 minutes before placing your glazed pecans around the perimeter and sprinkling crushed red pepper flakes and salt over the top, if desired. Chill the tart in the refrigerator for 3 hours, and let it sit at room temperature for about 10 to 15 minutes before serving.

More of an oatmeal raisin person? I got you, fam. Omit the chips, mixing in 1 cup of old-fashioned rolled oats and ¾ cup raisins instead. Add 1 teaspoon ground cinnamon along with the flour in the filling, whisking to distribute it equally throughout the dry mix.

Chocolate Chip Cookie Pie

Makes 8 to 10 servings

Borrowing the very best, most crave-worthy parts of the classic chocolate chip cookie, this pie has the perfect hint of vanilla, the comforting sweetness of caramelized brown sugar, and just the right amount of chocolate. Soft and gooey straight out of the oven, it is like childhood memories all stuffed into a flaky crust. Enjoy a nostalgic bite of warm cookies just like Mom would make, fresh out of the oven, in a more substantial serving fit for an adult appetite.

CRUST:

¼ cup vegan butter
4½ ounces (½ cup + 2 tablespoons) vegan cream cheese
1⅓ cups all-purpose flour
¼ teaspoon salt
1½ teaspoons apple cider vinegar
1–2 tablespoons unsweetened nondairy milk

COOKIE DOUGH FILLING:

2 tablespoons whole flaxseeds
1 cup all-purpose flour
¼ teaspoon baking powder
½ cup granulated sugar
½ cup dark brown sugar, firmly packed, or coconut sugar
10 tablespoons vegan butter
1 teaspoon vanilla extract
¼ teaspoon salt
8 ounces (1⅓ cups) semisweet chocolate chips

For the crust, combine the butter, cream cheese, and flour in a medium bowl, using a fork or pastry blender. Alternately, this may be done in a food processor, pulsing to roughly incorporate. The mixture should reach a consistency similar to coarse crumbs. Being careful not to overwork the dough, mix in the salt and vinegar. Slowly drizzle in the nondairy milk while continuing to stir; add just enough to bring the dough together into a cohesive ball. Turn the dough out onto a flat surface, pressing it together into one cohesive ball with your hands. Wrap it in plastic wrap and refrigerate for at least one hour.

Once chilled, roll the dough out onto a well-floured surface, forming a circle that is approximately 12 inches in diameter. Gently move the circle into a 9-inch round pie pan and flute the edges as desired. Loosely cover the crust in plastic wrap and return it to your refrigerator while you assemble the filling.

Preheat your oven to 325°F (160°C).

For the filling, grind the flaxseeds into a fine powder, and add it to a large bowl, along with the flour, baking powder, and both sugars. Melt the butter and stir it into your dry ingredients. Follow with the vanilla, salt, and chocolate chips, stirring thoroughly to combine. This mixture will be very thick, just like your standard cookie dough.

Remove your crust from the refrigerator and press the cookie dough filling evenly into it with a spatula. Bake for 55 to 60 minutes, until the center appears to have puffed up a bit and the crust is golden brown. Let the pie cool for at least 30 minutes. If you let it cool all the way down to room temperature, reheat individual slices in the microwave and serve warm.

Coconut Custard Pie

Makes 8 to 10 servings

Coconut fans, lend me your forks! Intensely flavored with coconut in no less than four different forms, the creamy coconut custard alone will make you swoon. In fact, should you find yourself pressed for time, feel free to skip the crust altogether and chill the filling in individual custard dishes for a simple tropical treat.

CRUST:

1 cup all-purpose flour
1 tablespoon sugar
¼ teaspoon salt
½ cup vegan butter
2–4 tablespoons cold water

COCONUT CUSTARD:

1 cup cooked white beans
1 cup full-fat coconut milk
1 cup granulated sugar
¼ cup coconut oil, melted
1 tablespoon all-purpose flour
1 teaspoon vanilla extract
1½ cups unsweetened shredded coconut
¼ cup unsweetened coconut flakes or chips, toasted

Put the lime in the coconut by adding 1 tablespoon lime zest when you want a little extra citrus kick. Though it's hard to resist the pun, orange or lemon zest could also liven up the basic combination quite nicely, too.

In a medium bowl, combine the flour, sugar, and salt. Add the butter and work it through with a fork or pastry cutter until the mixture resembles coarse crumbs. Alternately, this may be done in a food processor, pulsing to roughly incorporate. Add the water, one tablespoon at a time, and continue working it gently with your hands until it comes together into a ball of dough. Press into a flat disk, cover with plastic wrap, and refrigerate until chilled, at least 30 minutes.

Remove the dough from the refrigerator and roll it out onto a lightly floured surface. Aim for a circular shape that is 1 to 1½ inches larger than your pie tin, and about ¼- to ⅛-inch thick. Very gently fold the circle in half and then in half again, so that you can lift it without tearing, and carefully unfold it into a 9-inch round pie pan. Cover any tears that might have occurred and flute the edges as desired. Set aside.

Preheat your oven to 350°F (175°C).

Using a food processor or blender, puree the beans until completely smooth. Add in the coconut milk and sugar, processing to combine. Melt the coconut oil and slowly drizzle it in while running the motor to emulsify. Incorporate the flour and vanilla. Finally, fold in the coconut flakes by hand and pour this mixture into your crust.

Bake for 40 to 50 minutes, until the crust is evenly browned and the filling appears to have risen a bit. The custard will still be wobbly in the center, but it will continue to set up as it cools, much like a cheesecake. Let the pie sit for at least an hour before sprinkling the toasted coconut on top and serving.

Ginger Dream Pie

Makes 8 to 10 servings

Fresh ginger, that gnarled and twisted rhizome languishing alongside other "exotics," doesn't get nearly enough love in American kitchens. Everyone has the dried powder on their spice racks, but the true impact of the piquant, pungent tuber is a whole different taste altogether. My passion for the subtropical, sweet spice knows no bounds, as is obvious by the abundance of all sorts of gingery ingredients tucked into my pantry, candy dishes, and refrigerator crisper at all times. Using a triple dose of ginger—candied, dried, and fresh—this chilled cream pie offers a tantalizing combination of hot and cold that still manages to taste refreshing thanks to a quick chill in the refrigerator.

GINGER CRUST:

½ cup vegan butter
⅓ cup granulated sugar
¼–½ cup crystallized ginger, finely
    minced
⅓ cup almond meal
½ cup all-purpose flour
½ cup whole wheat flour
1 teaspoon ground ginger
1 teaspoon lemon juice

GINGER CREAM FILLING:

2 (12-ounce) packages firm silken
    tofu
1 tablespoon fresh grated ginger
1½ cups confectioners' sugar
2 tablespoons cornstarch
2 teaspoons ground ginger
1 teaspoon baking powder
¼ teaspoon salt
2 tablespoons vanilla extract

Preheat your oven to 350°F (175°C) and lightly grease and flour a 9-inch round pie pan.

In a medium bowl, cream together the butter and sugar until soft and fluffy. Ensure that the crystallized ginger is very finely minced, with no large chunks, as it can become overwhelming in such concentrated large doses. Adjusting the amount (¼ to ½ cup) to your personal preference and spice tolerance, add the crystallized ginger to your bowl along with the almond meal, flours, ground ginger, and lemon juice. Stir so that the mixture is thoroughly combined, but still somewhat crumbly. Press this into the bottom of your prepared pan and bake for 13 to 16 minutes, until it just begins to brown around the edges.

For the filling, begin by draining any excess water from the tofu. Add the tofu to your food processor or blender, along with the fresh grated ginger, and process it until smooth. In a small bowl, combine the sugar, cornstarch, ground ginger, baking powder, and salt. Add this dry mixture to the pureed tofu, and process again. With the motor running, drizzle in the vanilla and continue processing until everything is fully incorporated. Pour this mixture into your prepared crust, smoothing the top with a spatula. Bake for 20 to 24 minutes, until slightly puffed and the top no longer appears shiny. The center may still be wobbly when it comes out of the oven, but it will continue to set as it cools.

Chill the pie thoroughly, for at least 2 hours, before serving, and sprinkle with additional crystallized ginger, if desired.

Harvest Pie

Makes 8 to 10 servings

While transitioning away from summer to autumn is always a struggle for me, there's still a whole lot to celebrate in welcoming the cooler months ahead, like crisp apples, tart cranberries, and glowing golden sweet potatoes. Venture outside of one-dimensional old recipes that only pay homage to one lonely produce pick and get a full taste of the season all in one forkful. Though ideal for gracing the festive Thanksgiving table, this pie is perfectly at home for any old day when the leaves turn brown and begin to drop.

SWEET MAPLE CRUST:

2½ cups all-purpose flour

½ cup whole wheat flour

½ teaspoon salt

¾ cup vegan butter, well-chilled or frozen

¼ cup maple syrup

3–5 tablespoons water

FRUIT FILLING:

1 large, sweet apple (such as fuji or gala)

½ teaspoon lemon juice

1 small sweet potato (about 8 ounces)

8 ounces whole cranberries, fresh or frozen

¾ cup dark brown sugar, firmly packed

¼ cup cornstarch

¾ cup chopped walnuts

¼ teaspoon salt

¼ teaspoon ground nutmeg

2 tablespoons vegan butter

Aquafaba, to assemble

For the crust, toss the flours, salt, and butter into a medium bowl, and combine them with a fork or pastry cutter. Alternately, this may be done in a food processor, pulsing to roughly incorporate. Continue blending until coarse crumbs develop and small pieces of butter are left intact. Mix in the maple syrup, followed by the water, adding just one tablespoon at a time until the dough comes together into a cohesive ball. You may need to work the dough with your hands as it becomes stiff. Divide the resulting dough into two even pieces, smooth them into round disks, and wrap each tightly with plastic wrap. Refrigerate the dough for at least 2 hours before proceeding.

Once the dough is thoroughly chilled, preheat your oven to 400ºF (205ºC). Take one of the disks and roll it out to about a ¼-inch thickness on a lightly floured surface. Carefully move the flattened round of dough into a lightly greased 9-inch round pie pan and patch any holes or tears that may have formed in that transition. Place the pan in the refrigerator while you assemble the filling.

Peel, core, and chop the apple into bite-sized pieces before tossing it into a large bowl with the lemon juice. Peel and dice the sweet potato in a similar manner before mixing it in as well. Add all the remaining ingredients for the filling, except for the butter, and stir gently to coat the fruit evenly with the dry ingredients. Remove the pie pan from the refrigerator and pour the fruit and nut mixture into your prepared crust. Cut the butter into very small pieces, and scatter the chunks atop your filling. Set aside.

(continued on next page)

Take your second disk of dough and roll it out in a similar fashion, but this time cut out shapes of your choice with a cookie cutter. Here's your chance to get creative! I like arranging an artful pile of leaves around the edge, adding veins and other details with toothpick impressions, but there's no right or wrong approach here.

Brush the exposed lip of the base crust with aquafaba, just a small patch at a time, before firmly but gently pressing the shapes in to adhere. Brush the exposed surface with additional aquafaba when everything is in place. Carefully slide the whole pie into your oven and bake for 10 minutes, and then lower the oven temperature to 350ºF (175ºC) without removing the pie. Bake for an additional 25 to 30 minutes, until the top crust pieces turn golden brown. Let cool before serving.

Mont Blanc Mini Tarts

Makes 6 mini tarts

To be perfectly honest, an "authentic" Mont Blanc is quite different from my interpretation. While the original begins with a base of meringue instead of a crust, this version is much easier to prepare and just as delicious. Concealing a smooth maple crème filling with a generous mound of sweet chestnut crème, it is a perfect treat for the serious sweet tooth. Even if it's not a very authentic rendition of the dessert first created in honor of a mountain in the Alps, topped with powdered sugar to complete the look of a snowy peak, it still makes for one fantastic tart.

ALMOND CRUST:

1¼ cups almond meal

2 tablespoon ground flaxseeds

2 tablespoons coconut sugar or dark brown sugar, firmly packed

¼ teaspoon salt

¼ cup vegan butter or coconut oil, melted

½ teaspoon almond extract

CASHEW CRÈME FILLING:

1½ cup raw cashews, soaked in hot water for 2–3 hours

1 cup pitted medjool dates, packed

½ cup plain nondairy milk

1½ teaspoons vanilla extract

CHESTNUT CRÈME:

10 ounces roasted, peeled chestnuts

1⅓ cups unsweetened nondairy milk, divided

⅔ cup maple syrup

1 tablespoon dark rum

1 teaspoon vanilla extract

Confectioners' sugar, to garnish (optional)

Preheat your oven to 350°F (175°C).

In a medium bowl, stir together the almond meal, ground flax, sugar, and salt. Drizzle in the melted butter or coconut oil along with the almond extract, mixing to combine. You should end up with a relatively homogenous and cohesive if slightly crumbly mixture. Distribute between six 3-inch round mini tart pans with removable bottoms, pressing it evenly up the sides and along the bottoms. Chill for 10 minutes before baking.

Bake the crusts for 10 to 12 minutes, until lightly brown all over. Let cool completely while you assemble the fillings.

Drain the cashews thoroughly before tossing them into your food processor or a high-speed blender, along with the pitted dates. With the motor running, slowly pour in the nondairy milk, followed by the vanilla extract. Pause to scrape down the sides of the container as need, incorporating all the ingredients into a silky-smooth blend. Transfer the resulting crème to the baked crusts, spreading it evenly into each one.

Meanwhile, for the chestnut crème, place the chestnuts, ⅔ cup nondairy milk, and maple syrup in a small saucepan over medium heat. Bring to a simmer and gently cook for 10 to 15 minutes, until the liquid has reduced to a thick syrup that coats the back of a spatula. The chestnuts themselves should appear candied and be fork-tender all the way through.

After thoroughly washing all parts of your food processor or blender, reassemble it and process the chestnuts until completely smooth. Add in the rum and vanilla, blending once more to

(continued on page 181)

incorporate. Slowly drizzle in the remaining nondairy milk while running the motor, taking your time to make sure that everything is completely and utterly silky-smooth. Any remaining chunks, no matter how small, will clog the nozzles of your piping tip and make the topping impossible to apply. Save yourself the frustration by taking an extra minute or two on this step!

Transfer the resulting chestnut crème into a pastry bag fitted with an angel-hair tip. Pipe the chestnut crème on top of the maple crème layer in a circular path, starting from the outside and working in, mounding it up as high as possible. Dust with confectioners' sugar just prior to serving, if desired.

It's much easier to simply buy shelled, roasted chestnuts, often found in the kosher section when not in season, but you can also roast your own if you happen to get them fresh. Preheat your oven to 400°F (205°C) and use a very sharp knife to cut an "X" into the flat side of each chestnut. Place in a single layer on a sheet pan and roast until shells begin to open and reveal the nut within; about 20 to 30 minutes, stirring after 10 minutes. Peel the shells while still warm.

Pink Lemonade Tartlets

Makes 24 tartlets

Just like the brilliant pink glasses of icy lemonade making a splash at picnics or backyard barbecues across the country, these two-bite treats offer a refreshingly tart taste of citrus, tempered by a light sweetness. However, these tiny tarts have a clear advantage over the competition, as they derive their rosy hue from nothing more outlandish than raspberry jam, as opposed to the mysterious chemical cocktail found in powdered drink mixes. Bake up a batch to sate your sweet tooth and quench your thirst for a bright, refreshing taste of summer any day!

CRUST:
6 tablespoons vegan butter
½ cup confectioners' sugar
1 tablespoon whole flaxseeds
2 tablespoons water
1½ cups all-purpose flour
¼ teaspoon salt

LEMON CUSTARD:
1 cup plain nondairy milk
2 tablespoons cornstarch
2 tablespoons seedless raspberry
   jam
⅓ cup confectioners' sugar
2 tablespoons lemon juice
1 tablespoon lemon zest

TO GARNISH:
½ cup fresh raspberries
Candied lemon slices, quartered
   (optional)

Preheat your oven to 350ºF (175ºC) and lightly grease two dozen mini muffin pans.

For the crust, begin by beating the butter and sugar in your stand mixer until light and creamy. Grind the flaxseeds into a powder with a spice grinder and blend them together with the water. Add the flax mixture into your mixer and blend well. Add half of the flour, mixing until it is completely incorporated. Follow with the other half of the flour along with the salt, mixing until smooth. If the dough is still crumbly, add up to 2 additional tablespoons of water, just until the mixture sticks together. Drop walnut-sized balls of dough into each prepared muffin tin and press the dough up the sides of the pan using your fingers or the end of a wooden spoon, to form the tartlet shells. Bake for 12 to 15 minutes, until lightly browned. Let the tartlet shells cool completely.

To make the filling, heat the nondairy milk in a saucepan over medium heat. Add in the cornstarch and whisk vigorously to prevent lumps from forming. Continue stirring, and in 2 to 4 minutes of even heating, the mixture should thicken significantly. Add the jam and sugar, stirring to dissolve. Remove the mixture from the heat and whisk in the lemon juice and zest. Spoon your pink lemonade filling into the tartlet shells and chill for at least an hour before serving. Garnish the tartlets with fresh raspberries and candied lemon slices if desired.

To make candied lemon slices, use the same technique as outlined in the recipe for Orangettes (page 217) but use small, thinly sliced lemons instead. The key is to keep the slices consistent, so use a mandoline to keep all the pieces about ⅛ of an inch thick, if possible. Remove all seeds before getting started, and cook very gently to prevent the delicate membrane from getting destroyed in the process.

Pumpkin Pecan Pie

Makes 8 to 10 servings

At last, a delicious resolution to the pumpkin vs. pecan pie battle. While I have never felt that either pie was worthy of all the hype, it appears they simply needed to be combined in order to achieve their full potential. Straight pumpkin pie strikes me as monotonous in texture and flavor, while standard pecan pie tends to be tooth-achingly sweet. However, when I brought them together in one crust, the two fillings seemed to accentuate one another's strengths, while diminishing any negative aspects. The pecans do have a more dominant presence, but a dollop of pumpkin crème topping allows both flavors to have an equal turn in the spotlight. Who says you can't make everyone happy?

Crust:
1½ cups whole wheat pastry flour
1 tablespoon granulated sugar
½ teaspoon salt
½ cup vegan butter
3 tablespoons plain nondairy milk

PUMPKIN FILLING:

1 cup pumpkin puree
⅓ cup granulated sugar
2 tablespoons plain nondairy milk
½ teaspoon ground cinnamon
¼ teaspoon ground nutmeg
¼ teaspoon ground ginger
2 tablespoons cornstarch

PECAN FILLING:

1½ cups pecan halves
⅔ cup maple syrup
¼ cup dark brown sugar, firmly
   packed, or coconut sugar
3 tablespoons cornstarch
1 tablespoon ground flaxseeds
½ teaspoon vanilla extract

To begin forming the crust, combine the flour, sugar, and salt in a medium bowl. Melt the butter and pour it over the dry ingredients. Follow with the nondairy milk and mix until everything comes together into a cohesive ball of dough. Move the dough into your prepared pie pan and press it gently into the bottom and up the sides using the palm of your hand. Flute the edges if desired. Let the crust chill in the refrigerator while you assemble the filling.

Preheat your oven to 350°F (175°C).

In a large bowl, combine the pumpkin puree, sugar, nondairy milk, and spices. Slowly sprinkle in the cornstarch while stirring vigorously, to prevent lumps. Smooth this filling into your chilled crust and return the pie pan to the refrigerator.

In a separate bowl, toss the pecans with the maple syrup, sugar, cornstarch, ground flaxseeds, and vanilla. Gently and evenly pour this pecan mixture over your pumpkin filling. Don't worry if it looks like a skimpy amount; it will rise to the occasion once completed.

Bake the pie for approximately 25 minutes, until the crust begins to brown. Lower the oven temperature to 300°F (150°C) and bake for an additional 10 to 15 minutes, making sure that all the exposed crust looks fully cooked and nicely browned. If it is darkening too quickly, cover the edges with a strip of aluminum foil to prevent burning. Let cool completely.

(continued on next page)

PUMPKIN CRÈME:

1 (14-ounce) can full-fat coconut
   milk
¼ cup vegan butter or coconut oil
¾ cup confectioners' sugar
½ cup pumpkin puree
2 tablespoons arrowroot powder
1 teaspoon agar powder
¼ teaspoon ground cinnamon
Lightly grease a 9-inch round pie
   pan.

To make the pumpkin crème, combine the coconut milk, butter or coconut oil, and sugar in a medium saucepan over moderate heat. Once the butter or oil has melted, whisk in the pumpkin, arrowroot, agar, and cinnamon, beating thoroughly to incorporate without any lumps at all. Cook until thickened and bubbles begin to break on the surface, 8 to 10 minutes. Turn off the heat and let cool for about 30 minutes, stirring periodically to prevent a skin from forming on top. If it is still too soft to pipe around the border, let this mixture sit in the refrigerator for a few minutes to chill and solidify. Pipe or drop dollops of the crème around the edge of your pie before serving.

Spiralized Apple Galette

Makes 6 to 8 servings

Tender, warmly spiced apples wrapped up in a flaky free-form piecrust is an easy sell, but not always such an easy endeavor. Power through that pile of crisp autumnal fruit by spiralizing them instead of chopping by hand, and you'll have a showstopping dessert hot out of the oven in no time at all.

CLASSIC PIECRUST:

1¼ cups all-purpose flour

1 teaspoon granulated sugar

¼ teaspoon salt

6 tablespoons vegan butter, chilled, cut into small pieces

1½ teaspoons lemon juice

1–2 tablespoons ice-cold water

SPIRALIZED APPLE FILLING:

1 pound (2 medium) tart apples (such as granny smith)

1 pound (2 medium) sweet apples (such as fuji)

1 tablespoon lemon juice

½ cup dark brown sugar, firmly packed, or coconut sugar

5 tablespoons arrowroot powder

1 teaspoon ground cinnamon

½ teaspoon ground ginger

¼ teaspoon ground cardamom

¼ teaspoon ground nutmeg

1 tablespoon unsweetened non-dairy milk

1 tablespoon turbinado sugar

The easiest, quickest way to make a traditional piecrust is to get a helping hand from your food processor. Some say this approach sacrifices flakiness in favor of convenience, but I don't believe that any of my pies have suffered as a result. If you have the equipment, my advice is to use it!

Place the flour, sugar, and salt in the bowl of your food processor and pulse to combine. Add the butter and pulse 6 to 8 times, until the mixture resembles very coarsely ground almond meal. A few small chunks of butter should remain visible, but nothing larger than the size of peas. Sprinkle lemon juice and the first tablespoon of water in while pulsing a few times to incorporate. If the dough holds together when squeezed, you're good to go. If it remains crumbly, keep adding water while pulsing, just a teaspoon at a time, until the dough is cohesive.

In case you don't have a food processor or just don't want to clean the darn thing afterward, the old-fashioned method is just as effective, if a bit more labor-intensive. Place the flour, sugar, and salt in a large bowl and use a pastry cutter or two forks to cut in the pieces of butter. A few small chunks of butter should remain visible, but nothing larger than the size of peas. Sprinkle lemon juice and one tablespoon of water into the bowl and stir well with a wide spatula. Sometimes it can be difficult to get the liquids properly incorporated, so it may be helpful to drop the formalities and just get in there to mix with your hands. If the dough holds together when squeezed, you're set. If it remains crumbly, keep adding water and mixing thoroughly, just a teaspoon at a time, until the dough is cohesive. Do your best not to overmix or overhandle the dough, as this will make it tough when baked.

(continued on next page)

Shape the dough into a rough round and flatten it into a disk about ½ inch in thickness. Wrap tightly with plastic wrap and stash in the fridge. Let chill for at least an hour, or up to a week.

Preheat your oven to 350ºF (175ºC). Line a baking sheet with a silicone baking mat or piece of parchment paper.

Spiralize the apples, discarding the cores and removing any errant seeds that might have fallen into the pile of curlicues. Very gently toss with lemon juice, sugar, arrowroot, and all the spices. Set aside.

Roll out the unbaked piecrust on a lightly floured surface to a thickness of about ⅛th of an inch, as round as you can possibly make it. Transfer the flat circle of crust to the prepared baking sheet and pile the spiralized and sugared apples in the center. Distribute the filling evenly in the middle, leaving a border of about 2 inches of the crust clean and clear. Fold over the sides to contain the filling, and lightly brush the exposed crust with nondairy milk. Sprinkle turbinado sugar evenly over the exposed crust.

Bake for 35 to 45 minutes, until the crust is golden brown, and the apple spirals are tender. Don't fret if some of the juices spill out of the sides, as there will still be plenty within. Let cool for at least 10 minutes before slicing and serve while still warm. Ice cream is optional as a pairing, but highly recommended!

MISCELLANEOUS MORSELS & DESSERTS

Berry Cherry Cocoa Crumble

Makes 10 to 12 servings

Warm, gooey, and far from photogenic, fruit crumbles make up for their homely looks with pure comfort in every shamelessly messy mouthful. Feel free to switch out the fruits depending on what you have on hand, as the basic formula is infinitely accommodating. Even if you only have canned fruits that are presweetened, go ahead and toss them in; just leave out the additional sugar in the fruit base. This family-style dessert is so easy to make that even a novice baker could pull it off with grace.

COCOA CRUMBLE:

½ cup vegan butter or coconut oil, melted

½ cup coconut sugar or dark brown sugar, firmly packed

¼ cup granulated sugar

¼ cup Dutch-process cocoa powder

¾ cup all-purpose flour

½ cup old-fashioned rolled oats

½ teaspoon instant coffee powder (optional)

¼ teaspoon salt

BERRY BASE:

1 pound strawberries

1 pound pitted and stemmed cherries

½ pound raspberries and/or blackberries

½ pound blueberries

2 tablespoons cornstarch

⅓ cup granulated sugar

Preheat your oven to 375°F (190°C).

For the crumble, mix together the melted butter or coconut oil with both sugars in a large bowl. Add in the cocoa powder, followed by the flour, rolled oats, instant coffee, and salt. Keep mixing until it comes together in loose crumbs of varying sizes. Set aside.

Wash, hull, and chop the strawberries into bite-sized pieces. Combine them with the cherries, raspberries and/or blackberries, and blueberries in a large bowl. Toss this fruit with the cornstarch and sugar before transferring the entire mixture into a 2-quart casserole dish. Spread the berries in as even a layer as possible. Sprinkle the prepared crumb topping over the entire surface.

Bake for 45 to 50 minutes, until the juices bubble up around the edges. Let the crumble cool for at least 10 minutes before serving.

For the fullest, greatest depth of flavor, prepare the crumble a day ahead, and allow the various ingredients to "marry" in the refrigerator overnight. Simply reheat the crumble in a 350°F (175°C) oven for 5 to 10 minutes to warm all the way through before serving. For the ultimate home-style treat, top each serving with a scoop of No-Churn Vanilla Bean Ice Cream (page 237).

> Either fresh or frozen fruit can be transformed into an equally delicious crumble but bear in mind that frozen fruit will need to be completely thawed and drained of excess liquid before using, to prevent the dessert from becoming too watery.

Brilliant Blueberry Parfaits

Makes 6 to 8 servings

Visually stunning and equally dazzling in luscious flavor, such charisma comes naturally to these elegant parfaits. Prepared in advance, waiting in the refrigerator and ready when you are, each tall delicious glass truly is parfait, "perfect" in French and in taste alike.

BLUEBERRY MOUSSE:

1 pound (about 3 cups) fresh or
  frozen blueberries
1 (12-ounce) package extra-firm
  silken tofu
1 tablespoon lemon juice
⅔ cup granulated sugar
1 teaspoon vanilla extract
1 tablespoon agar powder
2 tablespoons water

MAPLE CRÈME:

1 (14-ounce) can full-fat coconut
  milk
¼ cup vegan butter or coconut oil
½ cup maple syrup
1 tablespoon vanilla extract
2 tablespoons arrowroot powder
1 teaspoon agar powder
Fresh blueberries for garnish
  (optional)

> If you're not feeling blue, don't let it get to you! Try using raspberries or blackberries instead to vary the fruity theme without losing an ounce of its original splendor.

If frozen, let the blueberries sit at room temperature or microwave briefly to thaw completely. Drain the tofu of any excess liquid and puree it in your food processor or blender until smooth. Drain away any juice from the berries before tossing them in with the tofu. Blend the two ingredients for 3 to 4 minutes, to fully combine them and achieve a smooth texture. Add in the lemon juice and sugar, and process just to mix them in. In a small dish, heat the agar with the water for 15 to 30 seconds in the microwave, just long enough to dissolve the agar and form a sticky, translucent jelly. Don't drag your feet at this stage: quickly get the agar mixture into your food processor or blender with the other ingredients and run the motor immediately, or the agar will solidify and create gummy lumps that will not dissolve. Once everything is completely mixed in, spoon the mousse into any clear glasses that you wish to serve it in. Let the mousse sit in the refrigerator for at least 2 hours to set.

After thoroughly chilling the mousse, prepare the maple crème by placing the coconut milk, butter or coconut oil, and maple syrup in a medium saucepan over moderate heat on the stove. Once the butter or oil has melted, whisk in the vanilla, arrowroot, and agar, beating thoroughly to incorporate the powders without leaving any lumps remaining. Cook until thickened and bubbles begin to break on the surface; 8 to 10 minutes. Turn off the heat and let cool for about 30 minutes, stirring periodically to prevent a skin from forming on top. If it is still too soft to hold its shape, let this mixture sit in the refrigerator for a few minutes to solidify.

Finally, pipe or drop dollops of the crème on top of your blueberry mousse. Top with fresh berries right before serving, if desired.

Cherry Chocolate Truffles

Makes approximately 24 truffles

Cherries and chocolate, supposed aphrodisiacs and staples in candy boxes the world over, must necessarily be sinfully indulgent, right? Far from it, these ambrosial bites require only four spare ingredients and no added sugar to taste positively decadent. Few desserts honestly qualify as "health food," but this one can be justified as a good source of antioxidants thanks to those two superfoods, right? Go ahead, enjoy these unexpectedly wholesome truffles with a clear conscience!

CHERRY CENTER:
1½ cups dried cherries
½ cup Dutch-process cocoa
   powder

CHOCOLATE COATING:
4 ounces dark chocolate, chopped,
   or ⅔ cup semisweet chocolate
   chips
1–3 tablespoons plain nondairy
   milk

Puree the cherries in your food processor until they become a smooth paste, pausing to scrape down the sides of the container as needed. Add in the cocoa powder and process again. Continue blending and soon enough the whole mixture should come together into a firm ball. Move this dough to a storage container on the counter and allow the flavors to develop overnight. You *can* continue working with the dough, if you are in a hurry, but I highly suggest you give it time to rest.

To make the truffles, scoop a small amount of dough and roll it into a ball in the palm of your hands. The size of each ball will dictate the final size of each truffle. I would suggest about 1 tablespoon of dough for the core, but you may choose to go larger or smaller. Repeat this process until the entire fruit base is used up.

Once you have the cherry centers ready to go, place the chocolate in a small, microwave-safe bowl. Melt the chocolate in the microwave in 30-second intervals, just until it stirs together smoothly with no lumps. Stir in the nondairy milk to your desired consistency. More nondairy milk will result in a higher ratio of center to coating and the coating will be softer, while less will give you a thicker chocolate shell that solidifies more.

Set a piece of parchment paper on a baking sheet in your workspace. Drop one cherry center into the chocolate at a time, rolling it around to completely coat. Once fully coated, drop each truffle onto the parchment. Let sit at room temperature and let dry for at least two hours. If you'd rather not wait, you can stash the truffles in your refrigerator or freezer to speed up the process.

Five-Minute Coconut Fudge

Makes 32 small squares

Devilishly dark and creamy, this fudge beats the chips out of the cloying original "Fantasy Fudge" made from the tooth-aching combination of sweetened condensed milk and marshmallow crème. This fudge has an intense chocolate flavor accented with a luscious tropical flair that ensures that even the smallest squares will satisfy your cravings. Dangerously quick and easy to whip up, it redefines the concept of instant gratification.

2 cups (12 ounces) semisweet
  chocolate chips
2 tablespoons vegan butter or
  coconut oil
½ cup full-fat coconut milk
2 cups confectioners' sugar
½ cup Dutch-process cocoa
  powder
½ teaspoon vanilla extract
¼ teaspoon salt
1 cup unsweetened coconut chips
  or flakes, toasted

Line an 8x8-inch square baking pan with aluminum foil and lightly grease.

In a large, microwave-safe bowl, combine the chocolate chips, butter or coconut oil, and coconut milk. Heat for 1 minute on full power and stir thoroughly until completely smooth. If a few stubborn chips refuse to melt, continue to heat and stir at intervals of 20 seconds, as needed.

Sift together the confectioners' sugar and cocoa powder, breaking up any clumps, before adding both to the bowl of liquid chocolate goodness. Next, add the vanilla and salt, stirring vigorously until thick, silky, and uniform.

Pour the mixture into your prepared pan. Smooth out the top and sprinkle coconut evenly over the entire exposed surface. Press the coconut gently into the fudge with the palm of your hand to make sure that it adheres. Chill for at least 30 minutes, or until fully set, before cutting into squares.

Never get bored with the same old fudge again! Over the years, I've made it a hundred different ways, always with resounding raves. Here are just a few of my favorite variations:

Tropical Fudge: Add ½ cup of diced dried pineapple and 1 teaspoon of orange zest right before incorporating the vanilla.

Pecan Pie Fudge: Add 1 teaspoon of ground cinnamon along with the vanilla extract. Omit the coconut topping, and instead press 1 cup of toasted pecans into the top.

Peppermint Crunch Fudge: Add 1 teaspoon of peppermint extract with the vanilla and stir in 4 crushed candy canes. Omit the coconut topping and sprinkle with 5 additional crushed candy canes instead.

Flaming Hot Peanut Brittle

Makes 1 pound of candy

Packed with some serious heat, this nutty candy is well suited for spice-lovers. Be sure to warn your friends before they dig in, as I have witnessed a couple of alarming reactions from those with less adventurous taste buds. This brittle can have some serious after-burn, a slow heat that builds with every crispy, crunchy shard, so take your time to savor or it might just bite back!

1 cup roasted, salted peanuts
½ teaspoon chili powder
½ teaspoon ground cinnamon
¼ teaspoon ground cayenne
   pepper
¼ teaspoon smoked paprika
⅛ teaspoon ground black pepper
1¼ cups granulated sugar
¼ cup water
¼ cup maple syrup
½ teaspoon baking soda

Lay a silicone baking mat or generous length of parchment paper on a flat working space near your stove.

Toss the peanuts and spices together in a small bowl and set aside.

Heat the sugar, water, and maple syrup together in a saucepan over medium heat, stirring until the sugar dissolves and the whole mixture comes to a steady boil. Stir continuously while cooking for another 5 to 8 minutes, until your mixture thickens and becomes light amber in color. If you have a candy thermometer handy, the temperature should be around 300°F (150°C) or when a small amount of the mixture dropped into a cup of cold water creates hard, brittle threads.

Quickly stir in the reserved peanuts and spices, coating all the nuts without burning them. Add the baking soda, remove the pan from the heat, and continue mixing vigorously. Once combined, immediately pour this mixture onto your silicone baking mat or parchment paper, quickly spreading it into a single layer of peanuts, before it begins to set up. Let it cool completely before breaking into pieces. Store your brittle in an airtight container.

Floral Petits Fours

Makes 40 to 48 Petits Fours

Named for their diminutive size, petit four literally means "small oven" in French. Although they have run the gamut from sweet to savory appetizers, what most people associate with them today are miniature layer cakes, filled with custard or jam, and topped with a sugary glaze, rolled fondant, or sheets of almond marzipan. The secret ingredient lending these dainty teatime snacks such a vibrant golden hue and moist crumb is pumpkin puree, believe it or not. Hidden deep within the tender sponge cake, it seamlessly replaces the typical half-dozen eggs without contributing a hint of squash flavor.

One batch of cake makes enough for all three flavors. If you'd prefer to make just one flavor, either triple the filling and glaze of your choice or reduce the cake by a third and bake it in a 9x9-inch square baking dish. At this size, it will be thin enough that you can simply cut out your layers as is without slicing it in half across the center.

GOLDEN SPONGE CAKE:

2 cups all-purpose flour
1 cup granulated sugar
2 teaspoon baking soda
1 teaspoon baking powder
½ teaspoon salt
1¼ cups plain nondairy milk
¾ cup pumpkin puree
⅓ cup olive oil
2 teaspoons apple cider vinegar
2 teaspoons vanilla extract

Chamomile-Lemon Filling, Glaze,
    and Garnish (recipes follow)
Lavender-Blueberry Filling, Glaze,
    and Garnish (recipes follow)
Pomegranate Rose Filling, Glaze,
    and Garnish (recipes follow)

Preheat your oven to 350°F (175°C) and lightly grease a 13x9-inch baking dish.

In a large bowl, thoroughly whisk together flour, sugar, baking soda, baking powder, and salt. In a separate mixing bowl, whisk the nondairy milk, pumpkin, oil, vinegar, and vanilla until smooth. Pour the wet mixture into the bowl of dry ingredients and stir until smooth.

Transfer your batter to the prepared baking dish and use your spatula to smooth it down in an even layer. Bake for 18 to 22 minutes, until the cake is golden brown all over and a toothpick inserted into the center comes out clean. Let cool completely.

While the cake is in the oven, go ahead and get started on the fillings and glazes. (See following recipes for details.)

Turn the completely cooled cake out onto a cutting board and slice it horizontally into 2 thin, equal rectangular layers. Cut each sheet of cake into small, even squares of either 1 inch or 1½ inches. If you have them, square cookie cutters can also be used to ensure consistency.

Proceed to follow the steps to prepare any or all of the flavors below. Each flavor variation makes enough to fill and glaze 1 batch of cake, so if you want to serve all three, make 3 times the amount of cake (and be prepared to feed an army!).

(continued on next page)

To assemble, carefully cut the filling of your choice into equal squares to fit the cake pieces. Use an offset spatula to move each filling square onto the cut top side of one square of cake, being very careful as it's somewhat fragile. Top each with another cake layer. Move the assembled mini cakes to a wire rack set over a rimmed baking sheet to await glazing and finishing.

Prepare the glaze by placing all ingredients in a medium bowl and whisking thoroughly to combine. The glaze sets quickly, so wait until you're ready to use it before getting started.

Pour the fresh glaze generously over each little cake, using a spatula to smooth and fill in any gaps, allowing that it will be thinner on the sides. Top each little cake with the suggested garnishes as artfully as you see fit.

Repeat this process with all of the pieces and desired flavors.

Let the petits fours rest at room temperature for 2 to 3 hours before serving to allow the glaze to set, but don't wait too long to enjoy; they're best eaten the same day and should be kept no longer than a day or two.

Chamomile-Lemon Filling, Glaze, and Garnish

CHAMOMILE-LEMON FILLING:

1 d'Anjou or Bartlett pear, peeled, cored, and diced
1 cup water
3 bags chamomile tea
1 tablespoons lemon juice
½ teaspoon lemon zest
¼ cup dark brown sugar, firmly packed, or coconut sugar
½ teaspoon agar powder

LEMON GLAZE:

2 cups confectioners' sugar
2 tablespoons light agave nectar
3 tablespoons lemon juice
¼ teaspoon ground turmeric

GARNISH:

Lemon zest
Candied lemon (page 183)

For the filling, line a 9x5-inch loaf pan with aluminum foil and lightly grease.

Place the chopped pear, water, and tea bags in a medium saucepan over medium heat. Bring to a boil, reduce to medium-low, and gently simmer for 10 minutes. Remove from the heat and cover, allowing the tea to steep for 10 minutes. Remove the tea bags and squeeze firmly to extract all infused liquid before discarding.

Transfer the tea and pears to a blender, followed by the lemon juice and zest, sugar, and agar. Puree, pausing to scrape down the sides of the container as needed, until smooth. Pour the puree back into the saucepan and place and over medium heat once more. Bring to a boil and continue to cook while stirring constantly for 2 minutes, taking care to scrape the bottom of the pot with your spatula to prevent the mixture from sticking.

Spread puree into your prepared loaf pan, tapping it lightly on the counter to even out the surface, and let cool to room temperature. Transfer the pan to your refrigerator and chill for at least 2 hours, until firm enough to slice. See Petit Four directions above for preparing the glaze and bringing all the components together.

Lavender-Blueberry Filling, Glaze, and Garnish

LAVENDER-BLUEBERRY FILLING:

⅔ cup blueberries, fresh or frozen and thawed
¾ teaspoon dried lavender
1 cup water
¼ cup granulated sugar
½ teaspoon agar powder

BLUEBERRY GLAZE:

2 cups confectioners' sugar
¼ cup freeze-dried blueberries, finely ground
2 tablespoons light agave nectar
3 tablespoons water

GARNISH:

Dried lavender
Fresh blueberries

For the filling, line a 9x5-inch loaf pan with aluminum foil and lightly grease.

Combine all the filling ingredient in a blender and puree until smooth. Pour the puree into a medium saucepan and place over medium heat. Bring to a boil and continue to cook while stirring constantly for 2 full minutes. Be sure to scrape the bottom and sides of the pot with your spatula as you go to prevent the mixture from sticking.

Transfer the thickened puree into your prepared loaf pan, tapping it lightly on the counter to even out the surface, and let cool to room temperature. Transfer the pan to your refrigerator and chill for at least 2 hours, until firm enough to slice. See Petit Four directions above for preparing the glaze and bringing all the components together.

Pomegranate-Rose Filling, Glaze, and Garnish

Makes 40 to 48 Petits Fours

POMEGRANATE-ROSE FILLING:

1 tart green apple, peeled, cored, and diced
1 cup 100% pomegranate juice
⅓ cup granulated sugar
½ teaspoon agar powder
¾ teaspoon rosewater

POMEGRANATE GLAZE:

2 cups confectioners' sugar
2 tablespoons light agave nectar
3 tablespoons 100% pomegranate juice

GARNISH:

Fresh or candied rose petals
Fresh pomegranate arils

For the filling, line a 9x5-inch loaf pan with aluminum foil and lightly grease.

Place the chopped apple and pomegranate juice in a medium saucepan over medium heat. Bring to a boil, reduce heat to medium-low, and gently simmer for 10 minutes, until the apples are fork-tender. Pour the resulting apple-pomegranate mixture into a blender, along with the sugar, agar, and rosewater. Thoroughly puree, pausing to scrape down the sides of the container as needed, until smooth. Pour your puree back into the same saucepan and place over medium heat once more. Bring to a boil and continue to cook while stirring constantly for 2 minutes, taking care to scrape the bottom of the pot with your spatula to prevent the mixture from sticking.

Spread puree into your prepared loaf pan, tapping it lightly on the counter to even out the surface, and let cool to room temperature. Transfer the pan to your refrigerator and chill for at least 2 hours, until firm enough to slice. See Petit Four directions above for preparing the glaze and bringing all the components together.

Gingersnap Pistachio Parfaits

Makes 6 to 10 parfaits

Crisp and invigorating as the frigid air on an icy winter's morning, gingersnaps are synonymous with the season for good reason. Crunching through the thin planks of spice-flecked biscuits can instantly evoke the warmth of the holidays, no matter the time or place. Though each gingery morsel would be delightful all alone, pairing them with a vivid green pistachio mousse turns this childhood treat into a spectacular parfait. The creamy base acts as a soothing foil to the lively cookies, heightened with spicy chunks of candied ginger in every spoonful. When you're done shoveling snow, dig into a much-deserved reward that will melt away the frightful conditions outside.

GINGERSNAP COOKIES:

1½ cups all-purpose flour

1½ teaspoons ground ginger

1 teaspoon ground cinnamon

½ teaspoon ground allspice

¼ teaspoon ground nutmeg

¼ teaspoon ground cloves

¼ teaspoon salt

⅛ teaspoon baking soda

½ cup coconut sugar or granulated sugar

¼ cup molasses

3 tablespoons olive oil

1–2 tablespoons plain nondairy milk

PISTACHIO MOUSSE:

½ cup toasted pistachios, soaked for 3–4 hours and drained

1 large, ripe avocado

1 cup fresh baby spinach, loosely packed

6 ounces extra firm silken tofu

¼ cup light agave nectar or maple syrup

1 tablespoon lemon juice

½ teaspoon orange zest

¼ teaspoon salt

The cookies will take the longest time to make, so start by preheating your oven to 300°F (150°C) and lining two baking sheets with silicone baking mats or parchment paper.

In either a large metal bowl or a stand mixer, whisk together the flour, spices, salt, and baking soda. While you can certainly bring this dough together by hand, it will require some vigorous stirring, so I would advise bringing out the heavy artillery if you have it!

Meanwhile, combine the sugar, molasses, and oil in a small saucepan and heat gently. Cook the mixture and stir gently, just until the sugar has completely dissolved. Pour the hot liquid into the bowl of dry ingredients, immediately followed by the non-dairy milk, and mix well. It will be very thick and somewhat difficult to mix, but give it all you've got and don't waste time; it will become harder to work with as it cools.

Turn out the dough onto a lightly floured surface, press it into a ball, and roll it out to about ⅛ inch in thickness. Cut it into your desired shapes with cookie cutters and transfer the cookies over to the silicone baking mat. Aim for smaller pieces around 1 inch to best fit comfortably into the parfaits, and don't worry about making everything look perfect. Go ahead and toss the scraps right on the sheet without shaping them, since you'll be crushing them into crumbs anyway.

Bake until the cookies are just barely browned around the edges, 15 to 18 minutes, depending on the size of your shapes. Let the cookies sit for a minute on the baking sheet before moving them over to a wire rack to cool.

(continued on next page)

TO ASSEMBLE:

Whipped Coconut Cream
   (page 243)
¼ - ½ cup candied ginger, roughly
   chopped
½ cup toasted pistachios

To make the mousse, place the soaked and drained pistachios in a high-speed blender along with your peeled and pitted avocado. Pulse to combine before switching over to top gear, pureeing to a creamy consistency. Pause to scrape down the sides of the container with your spatula as needed. If you only have a basic blender or food processor, allow an extra 5 to 10 minutes to ensure that mixture is perfectly smooth.

Add in the spinach, tofu, agave or maple syrup, lemon juice, orange zest, and salt, blending again to combine. Continue blending until there are no visible pieces of spinach remaining and the mixture is entirely homogeneous.

When you're ready to assemble the parfaits, spoon the mousse into 6 to 10 small glasses, depending on how many mouths you'd like to feed. Take any scraps and extra cookies and toss them into your food processor, roughly crushing them into a pebbly consistency. When you have about 1 cup of crumbs, toss in the candied ginger, as much or as little as you like, along with the pistachios. Distribute the crunchy topping equally between your glasses.

Finish each parfait with a dollop of Whipped Coconut Cream, and don't forget to crown each with a perfect little gingersnap cookie! Bonus points if you can fashion yours to look like a miniature Christmas tree.

Serve right away or the cookies will begin to soften. Keep all components separate and assemble no more than 2 to 3 hours in advance if you'd like to prepare this dessert ahead of time.

Green Tea-ramisu

Makes 8 servings

East meets west for a Japanese spin on a cherished Italian invention. Tiramisu, replete with ladyfingers dipped in espresso and liqueur, layers of sweetened mascarpone cheese, and a dusting of bitter cocoa, has only been around since the 1960s, as timeless though it seems. Evolving with modern tastes, it's only sensible to continue that natural progression with some fresh flavors. Whisking up a strong brew of earthy matcha instead of dark roasted coffee beans, it makes a compelling argument that green is the new black. If you haven't yet tried sake, a Japanese rice wine, let this sweet introduction prove its subtly complex, rather than brash, booziness that other spirits might impart. Skip the fussy ladyfingers while you're at it, because it's infinitely easier to assemble these essential elements with a cake.

SPONGE CAKE:

1 cup plain nondairy milk
1 teaspoon apple cider vinegar
2 tablespoons vegan butter
⅔ cup granulated sugar
2 tablespoons olive oil
1 teaspoon vanilla extract
1½ cups all-purpose flour
1 teaspoon baking powder
½ teaspoon baking soda
¼ teaspoon salt

MATCHA SYRUP:

½ cup water
¼ cup granulated sugar
½ cup sake
1 teaspoon matcha powder

MATCHA CRÈME:

3 cups raw cashews, soaked for
    3–4 hours and drained
½ cup granulated sugar
¼ cup plain vegan yogurt
2 tablespoons sake
2 teaspoons matcha powder
1 teaspoon vanilla extract
¾ cup full-fat coconut milk
¼ cup coconut oil, melted

Preheat your oven to 350°F (175°C) and lightly grease an 8x8-inch square baking pan.

In a small bowl, combine the nondairy milk with the vinegar and set aside. In your stand mixer, cream together the butter and sugar. Add in the oil and vanilla, while mixing and scraping down the sides of the bowl to ensure that everything is incorporated. In a separate bowl, sift together the flour, baking powder, baking soda, and salt. Alternately add the dry ingredients and the acidulated milk into your stand mixer, mixing just until it all comes together. Be careful not to overmix and develop the gluten, as it may make the cake tough. Pour the batter into your prepared pan and bake for 24 to 28 minutes, until a toothpick inserted into the center of the cake comes out clean. Let cool completely.

For the matcha syrup, bring the water and sugar to a boil in a saucepan on the stove. Maintain a steady boil for 2 to 3 minutes, stirring occasionally, until the granules have all dissolved. Remove the sugar syrup from the heat and add the sake and matcha. Whisk vigorously in order to beat out any clumps of powdered tea. Let the syrup cool for at least 10 minutes.

Prepare the crème by placing the soaked and drained cashews in a high-speed blender along with the sugar, yogurt, sake, matcha, and vanilla. Begin to blend on low speed, using the tamper to press the nuts toward the blades until they're largely broken down and can keep moving without additional help. Slowly

(continued on page 209)

pour in the coconut milk and melted coconut oil, ramping up the motor until it's at the highest setting. Continue to process until the mixture is completely silky smooth, pausing to scrape down the sides of the container with your spatula as needed. If you don't have a high-speed blender, you can also do this in your food processor, but the texture might be a bit coarser.

Now, you're ready to begin constructing your tiramisu! Turn the cake out of the pan and slice it in half horizontally, resulting in two thin 8-inch squares. Use a sawing motion and a serrated knife to achieve a clean cut. When separating, be careful moving the layers so they don't crumble. If they do break in half, just use the pieces together as you would have with the whole slice. Line the now empty pan with a sheet of parchment paper; this will act as a sling to help remove the dessert later on.

Return the bottom piece to the pan and lightly brush the top with half of the syrup. Smother that with half of the matcha crème, applying it in an even layer that goes right to the edges. Place the other half of the cake on top, with the cut side facing up, and press it down lightly to keep the filling flush. Brush all over with the remaining syrup and spread the last of the matcha crème over all of that. Smooth the surface with a spatula (it will probably come right up to the top of the pan) and cover with plastic wrap. Chill for at least 2 hours.

To serve, top with a light sprinkling of additional matcha, if desired, and cut into 8 equal rectangles. Enjoy with a hot cup of tea!

"Culinary grade" matcha is typically recommended for cooking and baking applications such as this, but to be perfectly honest, that's only because it's of such low quality that you would be sorely disappointed to drink it straight. While it's more affordable pound for pound, you may need to use more of it to have the same impact. Adjust your measures to taste if needed, but ideally, just go with the good stuff ("ceremonial grade") to begin with.

Hazelnut Ravioli

Makes 24 to 30 small pastries

Whether entertaining friends or sharing a romantic evening for two, this sweet finale will definitely end the event on a high note! If working with phyllo dough isn't your cup of tea, you could easily substitute a sheet of puff pastry instead, though the results won't be quite as delicate or ephemeral.

HAZELNUT RAVIOLI:
1 package frozen phyllo dough
1 cup toasted hazelnuts or
⅔ cup hazelnut butter
⅓ cup vegan cream cheese
1 tablespoon Dutch-process
cocoa powder
2 teaspoons instant coffee
powder
1 teaspoon vanilla extract
¾ cup confectioners' sugar

HOT FUDGE SAUCE:
6 ounces (about 1 cup) semisweet chocolate, chopped
¾ cup full-fat coconut milk
1 teaspoon vanilla extract

TO SERVE:
½ cup toasted hazelnuts
(optional)

Thaw the phyllo dough completely before beginning. Once ready, preheat your oven to 375ºF (190ºC) and line two baking sheets with silicone baking mats or parchment paper.

In your food processor, grind the whole hazelnuts for a good 5 to 10 minutes, until they break down into a smooth paste. If starting with hazelnut butter, simply toss it into the machine and it's good to go. Mix in the cream cheese, cocoa powder, coffee powder, vanilla, and sugar. Blend until fully combined and fluffy.

Lay out the phyllo dough on a flat surface. Take 5 sheets at a time and cover the rest loosely with a lightly dampened towel. Cut the rectangle of dough you are working with in half horizontally, and then in thirds vertically, so that you end up with 6 even squares. Spoon about one tablespoon of the filling into the center of each square. Lightly moisten the bottom two edges with a fingertip dipped in water and fold the phyllo over to create a triangle. Press the edges down firmly to make sure the seal is solid. Move the triangle over to a baking sheet, and repeat with each of the remaining squares. Continue taking 5 sheets at a time, cutting and filling them, until you run out of both components. Always cover the phyllo that is not in use so that it doesn't dry out. Bake the ravioli for about 10 minutes, until they become nicely browned on the surface.

To make the hot fudge sauce, place the chocolate in a medium bowl. Heat the coconut milk in the microwave in a microwave-safe container for about 1 minute and pour it over the chocolate. Let everything sit for about a minute, allowing the chocolate to melt, and stir until completely smooth, then stir in the vanilla. Either pour the chocolate sauce into a dipping bowl to serve warm alongside your ravioli, or drizzle the baked parcels liberally just before serving. Sprinkle additional toasted hazelnuts on top, if desired.

Matcha Latte Freezer Pops

Makes 5 to 6 freezer pops

Unabashed lover of green tea that I am, these vibrant, grassy green popsicles are in constant rotation on my list of easy snacks come summertime. If you are feeling particularly indulgent, go ahead and splurge on real vanilla beans. Split and scraped into the base, they add amazing complexities that accentuate the matcha. To change up the taste altogether, use a pinch of lemon zest in place of the vanilla for a delicious citrus twist. My very favorite modification, however, is to add a few drops of peppermint extract, which kicks the refreshment factor up to 11.

1¼ cups plain nondairy milk
½ cup confectioners' sugar
1½ tablespoons cornstarch
2 teaspoons matcha powder
½ teaspoon vanilla extract

In a small saucepan over medium heat, whisk together the nondairy milk, sugar, cornstarch, and matcha until the powders are fully incorporated. Bring the mixture up to a boil, whisking the whole time. At this point, the mixture should have thickened considerably. Remove from the heat, stir in the vanilla, and allow it to sit for 5 minutes. Pour into ice pop molds or small paper cups. Allow the mixture to cool to room temperature before inserting popsicle sticks and moving the molds into the freezer, where they should sit for at least 8 hours to fully freeze.

If you have trouble getting the freezer pops out of the molds when they are ready to be eaten, simply dip the outside of the mold into a cup of warm water for a few seconds. The freezer pops should loosen enough to be easily removed.

Matzah Toffee

Makes 2 pounds of candy

Celebrating my first Passover as a vegan, I quickly discovered, to my great dismay, that there were absolutely no good recipes for plant-based and kosher sweets. Thankfully, a quick revamp of an old family favorite not only fit the bill, but also garnered rave reviews. An indispensable staple ever since then, it's every bit as essential to the occasion as those luminous bowls of matzo ball soup.

4–5 sheets matzah, to fit pan
1 cup vegan butter
1 cup dark brown sugar, firmly packed
¼ teaspoon salt
12 ounces (2 cups) semisweet chocolate chips
⅓ cup sliced almonds (optional)
¼ teaspoon flaky sea salt (optional)

Preheat your oven to 450°F (230°C) and line a 15x10-inch jelly-roll pan, or other shallow pan, with matzah sheets. Arrange them to cover the bottom evenly, overlapping just slightly; you may need to break them to do so.

In a saucepan over medium heat, melt the butter, brown sugar, and salt together, bringing them to a slow boil. Maintain a gentle boil without stirring for 3 to 5 minutes, until the mixture becomes thick enough to coat the back of a spoon. Pour the molten sugar mixture over the matzah and spread evenly. Bake in the oven for 4 minutes and remove carefully.

Sprinkle the chocolate chips on top of the matzah, then return the pan to your oven for another 30 to 60 seconds. After it comes out of the oven for this second time, use a flat, heat-safe spatula to gently spread the melted chocolate so that it covers the top as completely as possible. Sprinkle evenly with sliced almonds and/or sea salt, if desired.

Let the matzah toffee cool to room temperature, leaving it undisturbed until it has completely solidified. Break into pieces and store in an airtight container.

Orangettes

Makes 48 to 64 candies

Few people think to compost their old orange peels, let alone save them for a second use, but with a little love and a touch of sugar, the zesty scraps may end up being even more delicious than the fruit itself! It takes some patience to extract any residual bitterness from the pith, but the payoff is worth the extra work. This same approach will allow you to salvage any other discarded citrus skins, such as grapefruits, lemons, and limes.

3–4 navel oranges
3½ cups water, divided
½ cup granulated sugar
3 ounces (about ½ cup) dark chocolate, chopped, or semisweet chocolate chips

There are many ways to remove the peel from the oranges. Some suggestions include using a vegetable peeler or grater, but I like to do it with a knife. To do it my way, begin by cutting the oranges into quarters. With the skin side down, cut right along the edge as close to the actual peel as possible and remove the edible innards. If there is still white pith left over on the inside of the peel, simply scrape that off with the knife. Cut the resulting clean peel into thin quarters, so that each orange produces 16 strips. You should now have a few nicely cleaned segments of orange, so take a break and have a snack, or toss them into a salad later!

Place the cleaned strips of peel in a small saucepan and pour in enough water to cover, about 1 cup. Bring the water to a boil and continue to cook for about 5 minutes. Drain the water, return the orange peel to the pan, and add a fresh cup of water. Bring back to a boil, cook for 5 minutes, and drain again. Repeat this process once more to leach out any residual bitterness.

Now you are ready to candy the rinds! Add the sugar and a final ½ cup of water to the peels, and boil over medium heat once more. Continue to cook until the excess water evaporates and all you have left is a thin coating of smooth sugar on each of the strips. Remove from the heat and immediately move the saucepan contents onto a silicone baking mat or parchment paper. Spread the pieces out so that they don't touch, before the sugar begins to cool and solidify. Let cool.

Once the coating has completely hardened, place the chocolate in a microwave-safe dish, and microwave in 30-second intervals to prevent scorching. Stir thoroughly after each heating until the chocolate is completely melted and smooth. Dip a piece of peel half way into the chocolate and return it to the silicone baking mat. Repeat this process with the remaining orange peels. Allow the orangettes to dry before storing them in an airtight container.

Pumpkin Toffee Trifle

Makes 15 to 20 servings

Piled high with several strata of cream, cake, and crunchy morsels all served up in one grand, family-style goblet, the trifle is the epitome of unpretentious decadence. It's suitable for fancy dinners, holiday gatherings, or even laid-back buffets and seasonal potlucks. Although it does take some patience to make, each separate element can easily be prepared ahead of time and assembled when you're ready. If candy making is not your forte, or you're simply more of a chocoholic than you are crazy for caramel, throw in 1 to 2 cups of chocolate chips in place of the toffee, for pumpkin chocolate perfection.

TOFFEE:

¼ cup vegan butter

2 cups dark brown sugar, firmly packed

½ cup water

Pumpkin Cake:

½ cup vegan vanilla yogurt

½ cup granulated sugar

½ cup dark brown sugar, firmly packed

1 cup pumpkin puree

½ cup olive oil

1 teaspoon vanilla extract

½ teaspoon lemon juice

1 cup all-purpose flour

½ cup whole wheat flour

1 teaspoon baking powder

1 teaspoon baking soda

2 teaspoons ground cinnamon

½ teaspoon ground allspice

½ teaspoon ground ginger

½ teaspoon salt

VANILLA PUDDING:

4 cups plain nondairy milk

1½ cups granulated sugar

3 tablespoons cornstarch

2 tablespoons arrowroot powder

2 tablespoons vanilla extract

To make the toffee, line a baking sheet with a silicone baking mat or piece of parchment paper. Heat the butter, brown sugar, and water together in a large saucepan over medium heat. It's very important to stir the mixture continuously once it comes up to a boil, as it could very easily boil over if left unattended. Once rapidly bubbling, cook the sugar mixture for 12 to 15 minutes, until it reaches 300°F (150°C) or when a small amount of the mixture dropped into a cup of cold water creates hard, brittle threads. At that point, immediately pour the liquid toffee onto the center of the prepared baking sheet, being careful not to pour so much in one spot that it spills over the edges. Let the mixture sit until it has completely cooled and solidified. Break the resulting toffee into bite-sized pieces and set aside.

Preheat your oven to 350°F (175°C) and lightly grease an 8x8-inch square baking pan.

In a large bowl, beat together the yogurt, both sugars, pumpkin, oil, vanilla, and lemon juice until everything is thoroughly combined. In a separate bowl, sift together the flours, baking powder, baking soda, spices, and salt. Slowly add the dry ingredients into the bowl of wet, stirring just enough to bring the batter together into a smooth, homogenous mixture. Pour your batter into the prepared pan and bake for 30 to 40 minutes. When done, the cake will be golden brown on top and pulling slightly away from the sides of the pan. Let the cake cool completely before cutting into bite-sized cubes. Set aside.

The last component for your trifle is the vanilla pudding, which is also probably the easiest. You're in the home stretch now! Begin by heating the nondairy milk in a large saucepan over medium heat. Whisk in the sugar and cornstarch together while the milk is still relatively cool, dissolving all the starch now to prevent lumps later. When the liquid begins thickening, whisk more vigorously and continue to cook for up to 5 minutes, until it takes on the consistency of pancake batter; it will thicken further as it cools. Remove the mixture from the heat, stir in the vanilla, and keep agitating it for a few additional minutes. Wait for the pudding to cool completely before assembling the trifle, or the toffee will melt. If you have the time to spare, refrigerate and chill the pudding in advance.

To put everything together, place half of the cake cubes in a trifle dish, in as even a layer as possible. Top this with half of the pudding, and then half of the broken toffee pieces. The rest of the cake follows, continuing the same pattern with the rest of the pudding on top of that, and the remainder of the toffee to finish. If you don't plan on serving it immediately, cover with plastic wrap and store in the fridge. Just bear in mind that the toffee will soften as it sits; it's still every bit as tasty, if less crunchy.

Sesame Chews

Makes 24 to 32 chews

These chewy candies were born out of sheer luck. Playing around in the kitchen one day with various sugars and add-ins left over from previous baking ventures, I had no idea what might result from the pot bubbling away on my stove. Luckily, the results were not some strange science experiment to be discarded at the end of the day, but a rather tasty, toothsome treat! An unusual flavor sensation to be sure, but you will be surprised by how well the ingredients play together in this unique candy.

½ cup coconut sugar or dark brown sugar, firmly packed
½ cup light agave nectar
1 cup toasted black and/or white sesame seeds
½ cup sliced almonds
½ teaspoon vanilla extract
¼ teaspoon ground cardamom
¼ teaspoon baking soda

Line a 4x8-inch loaf pan with aluminum foil and grease well.

In a medium saucepan, heat the sugar and agave nectar together slowly, until the sugar dissolves and the mixture comes to a boil. Add in your seeds and nuts, stirring continuously while cooking for 4 to 5 minutes. When the mixture reaches 250°F (120°C), which is also known as the hard ball stage in candy making, remove the pan from the stove. Add in the vanilla, cardamom, and baking soda, stirring vigorously until everything is combined and the candy has lightened slightly in color and texture.

Pour the liquid candy into your prepared baking pan and resist the urge to spread it out manually. Once it goes into the pan, do not touch it for at least 30 minutes. After that time has elapsed, move it into the refrigerator to finish setting up, for about an hour. To cut the chews, remove the full strip from the foil and use a heavy knife that is long enough to cover the whole length in one slice. Press straight down, rocking the knife back and forth if it needs more persuasion, but do not saw.

The chews may stick together due to humidity, so it is best to wrap them separately in squares of parchment paper. Store in an airtight container in a cool place.

Trigona

Makes 24 triangles

Appeasing my father's sweet tooth has always been a challenge. While he loves sugar in its most pure and concentrated form, a connoisseur of all candies, most baked goods don't hold the same allure. If one exception could be made, however, it would be for baklava. Sticky with syrup, innumerable layers of flaky phyllo join in nutty harmony, straddling the line between dessert and confection. Trigona is simply a variation on the more commonplace baklava, trading walnuts and honey for pistachios and maple syrup. Though the assembly can be a bit time-consuming, the results are always worth your patience.

1 package frozen phyllo dough, thawed
1 pound shelled pistachios
½ cup granulated sugar
1 teaspoon ground cinnamon
1 cup vegan butter, melted
1½ cups maple syrup

Thaw the phyllo dough completely before beginning. Once ready, preheat your oven to 300°F (150°C) and lightly grease a 9x13-inch baking pan.

Very briefly process the pistachios in your blender or food processor to grind them down into a coarse meal, but keep the mixture very rough and chunky. In a large bowl, mix together the ground pistachios, sugar, and cinnamon.

Cut (or tear) the phyllo so that it will fit into the bottom of your prepared baking pan. It is okay if the pieces overlap a little. Begin by laying down one sheet and brushing the pastry with melted butter. Add another sheet of phyllo once the first is lightly but thoroughly coated. Brush the second sheet with butter. Repeat these steps up to 4 times to create a phyllo layer; the exact number is up to you. After applying the butter to the last sheet in your first phyllo layer, sprinkle it evenly with the pistachio mixture. Repeat the entire process to create a second layer of phyllo, followed by another layer of the pistachios. Continue this pattern until you run out of the dry ingredients, ending with a layer of buttered phyllo on top.

Before placing the trigona in the oven, precut the little triangles, or, if you are not feeling so handy with a knife, little squares are just fine. Bake for 70 to 80 minutes, until golden brown and slightly crispy-looking, but watch to make sure that the edges don't get over-toasted.

Gently warm the maple syrup, either on the stove or in the microwave, and pour it over the baked pastry. Allow the trigona to cool for at least one hour, then recut, and serve.

PANTRY STAPLES, COMPONENTS & ACCOMPANIMENTS

Apple Butter

Make about 1 quart

Apple butter, a humble spiced preserve, has nothing to do with any dairy additives, contrary to what the name might suggest. Naturally vegan and much loved across the country, it's easy to find in just about any grocery store. Unfortunately, like most other mass-produced jams and jellies, it's typically composed of more sugar than fruit. Seeking an option focused on flavor rather than pure sweetness, I decided to take things into my own hands. The process is easy enough for a complete beginner to master on the first try, even if you've never considered jamming before. Just make sure you have plenty of time before you light up your stove because it's not exactly a "quick fix" recipe.

6 cups unsweetened applesauce

12 ounces (1½ cups) frozen no-sugar added apple juice concentrate, thawed

2 tablespoons ground cinnamon

1 teaspoon ground allspice

½ teaspoon ground cloves

½ teaspoon salt

Combine all the ingredients in a large, heavy saucepan over medium heat on the stove. Whisk thoroughly to incorporate all the spices without any clumps remaining and bring to a boil. Reduce the heat to low, keeping the mixture at a gentle simmer. Continue to cook, uncovered, stirring periodically to make sure that nothing sticks to the bottom of the pan. Be patient as it will take anywhere from 2 to 4 hours to properly reduce by about half, to a thick, spreadable, jammy consistency. When finished, it will be considerably darker in color and coat the back of a spoon richly.

Let cool for at least 30 minutes before packing into glass jars and sealing tightly. When completely cool, store in the fridge for up to two weeks. This apple butter is low in acidity and thus difficult to properly can without extensive equipment, so it isn't shelf-stable. That just means you need to slather it on thick and eat it faster, which shouldn't be too much trouble!

Apples aren't the only fresh autumnal delights to harvest from the orchard. Go ahead and pump-kin it up! Instantly convert this seasonal schmear into Pumpkin Butter by trading the applesauce for 1 (14-ounce) can of pumpkin puree. Replace the allspice with nutmeg to get that classic freshly baked pumpkin pie flavor.

Chocolate Wafer Cookies

Even if you just need a solid base to build your cheesecake on, going the extra mile to make your own cookie crumbs can catapult your creations to a new plane of dessert divinity. That said, these chocolate wafers are deceptively addictive, so they may turn into the main event by themselves. Dress them up with a quick dip into melted chocolate, or smear a dab of vanilla frosting between two to make your own Oreos in an instant. If you can resist the temptation though, go ahead and toss them into your food processor when completely cool and pulse until finely ground to create the very best cookie crusts you've ever tasted.

1 cup vegan butter
1¼ cups granulated sugar
1¾ cups all-purpose flour
1 cup whole wheat flour
1 cup Dutch-process cocoa powder
½ teaspoon salt
½ teaspoon baking powder
⅓ cup cold coffee
1 teaspoon vanilla extract

Use your stand mixer to thoroughly cream the butter and sugar together. In a separate bowl, sift the flours, cocoa powder, salt, and baking powder, stirring well to combine. Add about half of the dry ingredients into the bowl, blending it until fully incorporated. Pour in the cold coffee and vanilla, along with the remaining flour mixture. Continue to mix until it forms into a smooth, homogeneous dough. Form the dough into a ball, flatten it out a bit, wrap in plastic, and chill for at least one hour before proceeding.

After the dough has had time to rest in the refrigerator, preheat your oven to 350°F (175°C). Line two baking sheets with silicone baking mats or parchment paper.

On a lightly floured surface, roll out the dough to about ⅛ inch in thickness. Use any cookie cutters you desire to shape the cookies, or if you plan on simply grinding them into crumb, make it easier on yourself and just use a pizza roller to quickly slice the dough into equally sized squares. Place them on prepared baking sheets.

Bake for 8 to 14 minutes, depending on the size. It's tough to judge when these cookies are done because they're so dark to begin with, but the edges should be firm, and the centers soft and slightly puffed up.

Cool completely on a wire rack before storing in an airtight container at room temperature.

Cream Cheese

Makes about 2 cups

Slightly salty, slightly sweet, cream cheese is one of the most versatile spreads around, and an absolute essential ingredient in my kitchen. Since it plays such a crucial role in desserts like cheesecake, quality really counts. Go the extra mile to make your own from scratch and instantly elevate your creations to the next level or enjoy it simply as a spread that will make even the average bagel sing.

Kombucha is an unconventional addition that you won't find in most recipes, but I've found that this fermented tea gives my schmear a perfectly tangy flavor. Seek out the most neutral variety available, such as an "original" flavor or a citrus blend.

1 cup raw cashews
½ cup slivered almonds
1 tablespoon apple cider vinegar
1 tablespoon lemon juice
1 tablespoon white miso paste
¼ teaspoon salt
½ cup kombucha

Place the cashews and almonds in a medium saucepan along with enough water to cover. Bring to a boil and simmer for 15 minutes. The nuts should have swollen a bit from absorption and have a more tender, "al dente" bite. Drain thoroughly and transfer to a high-powered blender or food processor. The better your equipment, the smoother your cream cheese will be, but anything you have can work nicely with an extra measure of patience.

Add in the vinegar, lemon juice, miso, and salt. Begin blending on low to break down the nuts, using the tamper to continue pushing the mixture into the blades, pausing periodically to scrape down the sides of the canister with a spatula. Once broken down to a crumbly, coarse meal, begin slowly streaming in the kombucha with the motor running. Turn up the speed to high and continue to puree, until completely smooth. Allow enough time for the blender or food processor to do its magic. Depending on your machine, it could take anywhere from 5 to 15 minutes to achieve the ideal silky-smooth texture.

Transfer to an airtight container and store in the fridge for up to 5 days. Kombucha is a living, fermented ingredient, so the cream cheese will continue to get tangier the longer it sits. Plan accordingly if you want to either downplay or highlight this distinctive flavor in your food or desserts.

Don't feel like baking this homemade delicacy into another dessert? Transform your basic cream cheese into a fancy flavored spread by blending up any of the following:

Garlic & Herb: Add 1 clove finely minced garlic, ¼ cup minced fresh parsley, 1 minced scallion, and ¼ teaspoon dried thyme.

Italian Tomato: Add ¼ cup finely minced sun-dried tomatoes, 1 tablespoon tomato paste, 2 tablespoons fresh minced basil, ½ teaspoon dried oregano, and ¼ teaspoon dried thyme.

Spicy Queso: Add 3 tablespoons nutritional yeast and 1 chipotle canned in adobo sauce.

Strawberry: Add ¼ cup seedless strawberry jam or preserves.

Maple Brown Sugar: Add 3 tablespoons dark brown sugar, firmly packed, 1 tablespoon maple syrup, and ¼ teaspoon ground cinnamon.

Lemon Poppy Seed: Add 2 tablespoons lemon zest, ¼ cup confectioners' sugar, and 1 tablespoon poppy seeds.

Easy Eggless Nog

Makes about 2½ cups

Quickly whip up your own nondairy nog at home when it's not in season to get a taste of the holiday spirit, any day of the year!

2 cups plain nondairy milk
½ cup raw cashews, soaked
    for 4–6 hours
¼ cup granulated sugar
¼ teaspoon ground nutmeg
¼ teaspoon kala namak (black salt)

Simply toss everything into your blender and thoroughly puree, until completely silky smooth. Pass through a fine-mesh strainer if desired, to further perfect the texture. Drink it straight, bake with it, or refrigerate for up to a week.

Graham Crackers

Makes about 30 to 40 squares, or 15 to 20 rectangles

Graham crackers are the building blocks of many a dessert, which is quite ironic because they were originally designed as an austere addition to a highly restrictive regimen, designed to cut down on rampant desire and other excesses. Reverend Sylvester Graham would likely be horrified by the sugary turn these originally bland wafer planks have taken in his absence, but the general public is all the better for it. Now a simple biscuit worthy of solo consumption, the only trouble is finding an option that doesn't contain honey. Scout out store brands for some "accidentally vegan" gems or get busy making an even better version from scratch. These won't cure you of any dietary evils, but they will instantly elevate your cheesecake crusts or simple s'mores to new culinary heights.

½ cup vegan butter

1 cup dark brown sugar, firmly packed

1 cup graham flour

1¼ cups all-purpose flour

½ teaspoon baking soda

½ teaspoon ground cinnamon

¼ teaspoon salt

¼ cup agave nectar or maple syrup

1 teaspoon vanilla extract

In your stand mixer, cream together the butter and sugar thoroughly, until fluffy and homogeneous.

Separately, sift together the flours, baking soda, cinnamon, and salt, before adding them all in to the bowl of the mixer. Start on low speed and begin to gently incorporate the dry goods into the butter and sugar mixture. Add in the agave or maple syrup and vanilla, and continue mixing until the dough comes together. Be sure to scrape down the sides of the bowl with your spatula periodically to mix in any pockets of unblended ingredients.

Once smooth and cohesive, pat the dough out lightly into a flat round, and divide it in two. Wrap up each half in plastic wrap, and chill for a minimum of two hours. If you can spare the time, I would highly recommend letting it rest overnight for the least sticky, most easily workable dough.

When you're ready to proceed, preheat your oven to 350ºF (175ºC), and line two baking sheets with parchment paper or silicone baking mats.

Roll out one half of the dough at a time on a lightly floured, clean surface, bringing it down to about ⅛ to to ¼ inch in thickness. Use a fluted pastry wheel or plain pizza cutter to slice the graham cracker shapes into either 2½-inch squares for s'mores or ice cream sandwiches, or 2½ x 5-inch rectangles to match the traditional dimensions. Carefully transfer the shapes with a flat spatula over to your prepared baking sheet and use a fork to evenly prick the cookies all over. Repeat with the second half of the dough. Afterward, gather up the scraps, reroll, and repeat once more.

Bake for 11 to 14 minutes for the squares, 13 to 16 minutes for the rectangles, until very lightly golden brown around the edges and no longer shiny on top. Let cool completely on the sheets. Store in an airtight container at room temperature.

No-Churn Vanilla Bean Ice Cream

Makes 1 scant quart

Plenty of low-tech methods exist for churning out frozen treats without fancy machinery, but let's be honest: few people, myself included, care enough to fuss with scraping around ice crystals or shaking a plastic bag of ice cubes all day, all for a few small bites of sweet satisfaction.

Your icy irritation ends here. All you need is a freezer, four ingredients, and an appetite. I would wager that you've already got two out of three already covered. The magic all lies in the natural richness of concentrated coconut cream, providing a light, scoopable structure without any further agitation, or irritation.

2 (14-ounce) cans full-fat coconut milk, chilled
1 cup confectioners' sugar
1 tablespoon vodka
2 teaspoons vanilla bean paste or extract

Carefully open the chilled cans of coconut milk without shaking them, scooping off the top layer of thick coconut cream that will have risen to the top. Save the watery liquid left behind for another recipe that calls for plain nondairy milk.

Returning to the task at hand, place the coconut cream in the bowl of your stand mixer and install the whisk attachment. Whip on high speed for about 3 minutes before slowly beginning to sprinkle in the sugar, just a few tablespoons at a time. Continue beating the mixture for up to 10 minutes, until light and fluffy. Finally, fold in the vodka and vanilla. Use as few strokes as possible to incorporate this final addition to keep the airy structure intact.

Spread the ice cream base into an airtight container and carefully move it into your freezer. Allow it to sit, undisturbed, for at least 6 hours before serving.

Orange Marmalade

Makes about 5 cups

Homemade marmalade is the crowning jewel atop any breakfast spread, shimmering in the sunshine like a genuine pot of gold. Bathe your whole kitchen with the aromatic perfume of fresh citrus with every new batch, as restorative as a walk in the orange groves themselves. There's a fine line between bitter and sweet, so I've carefully calibrated the balance between zest and sugar. It's a labor of love to remove the harshly astringent pith, but always worth the effort. While you can always buy marmalade for a quick fix, it may be tough to go back after making it from scratch.

4 pounds (about 8–10)
   medium oranges
2½ cups water
½ cup lemon juice
5 cups granulated sugar

Add a whole new dimension of flavor your jam to really bring it to the next level. Consider adding any or all of the following along with your fruit: 2 tablespoons fresh ginger, finely grated; 1 vanilla bean, split and seeds scraped; 1 tablespoon lemon zest; 1 tablespoon orange blossom or rose water; 1 teaspoon ground black pepper.

Thoroughly scrub and dry the oranges before beginning. Use a very sharp paring knife to slice away the outer peels, removing only the brightly colored zest. Leave behind the white pith, which is incredibly bitter and unpalatable. If necessary, go back over your cut peels and shave away any pith that remains. Slice the clean zest into thin, short ribbons and set aside.

Returning now to the naked oranges, remove the thick layer of white pith left behind. Thinly slice the fruits about ¼-inch thick, membrane and all, removing any seeds you might encounter.

Combine the zest, innards, water, and lemon juice in a large heavy pot and bring to a boil.

Meanwhile, stash a small plate in the freezer to chill. This may sound strange, but it will help determine when the marmalade is thick enough to set properly. Have three pint-sized jars, or one quart and one half-pint jars, cleaned and ready to receive the jam, set nearby the stove so you don't need to travel too far with a hot pot.

Reduce the heat to a simmer and cook the mixture, stirring frequently, until the peels are translucent, and the liquid has reduced by at least ¾. Be patient, as this may take as long as 60 minutes. Add the sugar and continue to cook for another 45 to 55 minutes, until the liquid has almost completely evaporated. To test the consistency, spoon a dollop onto the chilled plate, let it sit for a minute, and drag a spoon through the mixture. When properly set, the marmalade will hold a clean path behind the spoon.

Remove from the heat, divide between the waiting jars, and seal immediately. Can the marmalade for long-term storage or keep in the refrigerator for quick consumption. Even if not traditionally canned, it will keep in the fridge for at least 4 to 6 months due to the high sugar content, if you can keep your spoon out of it that long, of course.

Raspberry Jam

Makes about 4 cups

When I was a teenager, summer break was just as busy as the school year. A part-time job kept me tied up for the better part of the day, but that never stopped me from going out with my dad afterward, to pick wild raspberries in the fading sunlight. No matter how tired we both were or how hot and humid the weather, we fearlessly beat back thorny vines to reap pounds upon pounds of fresh, plump berries, shimmering like red rubies in our juice-stained hands. We picked until it was too dark to see, reaping incredible yields beyond what any reasonable family of four could consume. Freezing, drying, and of course, jamming was the only solution after we had stuffed ourselves silly. This simple formula works just as well for blackberries, blueberries, or strawberries if you'd prefer, but raspberries will always have a special place in my heart, as well as my stomach.

4 cups raspberries, fresh or frozen
   and thawed
3 cups granulated sugar
2 tablespoons lemon juice
1 teaspoon vanilla extract

Place the berries in a large saucepan over high heat, mashing them roughly with a sturdy wooden spoon or potato masher as they begin to warm. Add the sugar and lemon juice, stirring roughly to incorporate while continuing to break down the fruit. Bring to a full rolling boil and cook for 10 to 15 minutes, stirring constantly.

When the jam is ready, it should reach about 220°F (104°C) on a candy thermometer or use the old-fashioned "spoon test": dip a cold metal spoon into the hot jam. Immediately lift it out and away from the steam and turn it horizontally. At the beginning of the cooking process, the liquid will drip off like a light syrup. The jam is done when the drops are very thick and run together before falling off the spoon.

Stir in the vanilla, ladle into glass jars, and seal immediately. Let cool completely before using.

Don't want to associate with a seedy crowd? Make your jam seedless by tossing the berries into your blender first and passing the puree through a fine-mesh strainer. Discard the solids and proceed with the recipe as written.

Whipped Coconut Cream

Makes about 2 cups

Simultaneously light and rich, a spoonful of lightly sweetened whipped cream is an ideal complement to almost every dessert. A breath of vanilla essence lends incredible depth, without stealing the spotlight from any potential headliner, no matter how soft-spoken, distinctive, or bold. With an eye toward the tropics rather than the farmlands, coconut cream easily stands in for dairy without any crazy stabilizers or demanding techniques necessary.

1 (14-ounce) can full-fat coconut milk, chilled
1 tablespoon granulated sugar
½ teaspoon vanilla extract

Carefully open the chilled can of coconut milk, being sure not to shake it, and scoop off the top layer of thick coconut cream that will have risen to the top. Save the watery liquid left behind for another recipe, such as a soup or a curry. Place the coconut cream in the bowl of your stand mixer and install the whisk attachment. Whip on high speed for about 3 minutes before slowly sprinkling in the sugar, just a little bit at a time. Continue beating the mixture for up to 10 minutes, until light and fluffy. Finally, fold in the vanilla extract. Use it in any recipe that calls for whipped cream, and pipe, dollop, or slather it on as artfully or generously as you desire.

Conversion Charts

Metric and Imperial Conversions

(These conversions are rounded for convenience)

Ingredient	Cups/Tablespoons/ Teaspoons	Ounces	Grams/Milliliters
Butter	1 cup/ 16 tablespoons/ 2 sticks	8 ounces	230 grams
Cheese, shredded	1 cup	4 ounces	110 grams
Cream cheese	1 tablespoon	0.5 ounce	14.5 grams
Cornstarch	1 tablespoon	0.3 ounce	8 grams
Flour, all-purpose	1 cup/1 tablespoon	4.5 ounces/0.3 ounce	125 grams/8 grams
Flour, whole wheat	1 cup	4 ounces	120 grams
Fruit, dried	1 cup	4 ounces	120 grams
Fruits or veggies, chopped	1 cup	5 to 7 ounces	145 to 200 grams
Fruits or veggies, pureed	1 cup	8.5 ounces	245 grams
Honey, maple syrup, or corn syrup	1 tablespoon	0.75 ounce	20 grams
Liquids: cream, milk, water, or juice	1 cup	8 fluid ounces	240 milliliters
Oats	1 cup	5.5 ounces	150 grams
Salt	1 teaspoon	0.2 ounce	6 grams
Spices: cinnamon, cloves, ginger, or nutmeg (ground)	1 teaspoon	0.2 ounce	5 milliliters
Sugar, brown, firmly packed	1 cup	7 ounces	200 grams
Sugar, white	1 cup/1 tablespoon	7 ounces/0.5 ounce	200 grams/12.5 grams
Vanilla extract	1 teaspoon	0.2 ounce	4 grams

Oven Temperatures

Fahrenheit	Celsius	Gas Mark
225°	110°	¼
250°	120°	½
275°	140°	1
300°	150°	2
325°	160°	3
350°	180°	4
375°	190°	5
400°	200°	6
425°	220°	7
450°	230°	8

Index

vanilla sugar, 26
vinegar
    apple cider, 2

W

waffles
    Hearty Granola Waffles, 47
walnuts
    Apple Spice Cake, 103
    Black Bottom Blondies, 67
    Carrot Cake Quinoa Cereal, 37
    Harvest Pie, 177–178
wasabi, 13
Wasabi Chocolate Cupcakes, 157
Whipped Coconut Cream, 243
    Berry Froyo Chiffon Pie, 162–163
    Cherry Cola Pudding Pie, 167
    Gingersnap Pistachio Parfaits, 205–206
Whoopie Pies, 99–100

Y

yeast. *See* nutritional yeast
yogurt, 13
    Apricot Biscotti, 62
    Berry Froyo Chiffon Pie, 162–163
    Black Bottom Blondies, 67
    Black & White Cookies, 64–65
    Butterscotch Blondies, 69
    Crumb-Topped Brownies, 75
    Green Tea-ramisu, 207–209
    Lemon-Lime Sunshine Bundt, 123
    Orange Dreamsicle Snack Cake, 133
    Plum-Good Crumb Cake, 143
    Pumpkin Toffee Trifle, 218–219
    Pup Cakes, 147
    Whoopie Pies, 99–100

Z

Zesty Cranberry Crumb Muffins, 57